Statistical Thinking for Data Scientists: Inference, Testing, and Regression

James Relington

DEDICATION

To those who seek knowledge, inspiration, and new perspectives—
may this book be a companion on your journey, a spark for curiosity,
and a reminder that every page turned is a step toward discovery.

AKNOWLEDGEMENTS

I would like to express my deepest gratitude to everyone who contributed to the creation of this book. To my colleagues and mentors, your insights and expertise have been invaluable. A special thank you to my family and friends for their unwavering support and encouragement throughout this journey.

Foundations of Statistical Thought

Statistical thinking is the cornerstone of modern data science. It offers a framework for understanding the variability inherent in data and guides rational decision-making under uncertainty. Long before the age of big data and machine learning, statisticians were developing principles that allowed people to draw meaningful conclusions from limited observations. These foundational ideas remain vital for today's data scientists, providing not only the mathematical tools to analyze data but also the philosophical grounding necessary to interpret results responsibly and effectively. At its heart, statistical thinking is about recognizing patterns, assessing reliability, and quantifying uncertainty.

The genesis of statistical thought lies in the challenge of making generalizations from incomplete information. Whether predicting outcomes in medicine, evaluating marketing strategies, or analyzing scientific experiments, data scientists rarely have access to the entire population of interest. Instead, they rely on samples—smaller, manageable subsets of the whole. The central concern, then, becomes how to make valid inferences from these samples, understanding that the data collected is subject to variability, chance, and potential bias. Statistical thinking teaches us to approach this problem not by seeking absolute truth but by embracing uncertainty and measuring it rigorously.

One of the first principles that statistical thinking instills is that variability is not noise to be eliminated, but a feature to be understood. Every dataset contains fluctuations—some stemming from the inherent randomness of the world, others from measurement error, and still others from underlying systematic influences. Rather than being discouraged by this variability, statistical thinkers seek to quantify and model it. They use probability distributions to represent possible outcomes and to assess how likely different events are. These distributions allow data scientists to describe both the expected behavior and the deviations from that behavior, forming the basis for almost every statistical method.

Another foundational concept is the idea of a population and a sample. The population is the full set of entities or events about which we wish to draw conclusions. A sample is the subset of that population we actually observe. Recognizing the distinction between these two is critical because the sample can never perfectly reflect the population. There is always a margin of error, a range within which the truth might lie. This awareness leads to the development of estimators, which are rules or formulas that help us approximate population parameters from sample data. A good estimator is unbiased, consistent, and efficient—properties that are formalized through rigorous statistical definitions.

Statistical thinking also emphasizes the role of randomness and the importance of random sampling. When samples are selected randomly, each member of the population has an equal chance of being included, which helps ensure that the sample is representative. This principle underpins the validity of many inferential techniques, such as confidence intervals and hypothesis tests. Randomness also plays a critical role in experimental design, where it helps to eliminate confounding variables and isolate the effects of interest. Without randomization, any conclusions drawn from the data are susceptible to hidden biases that can distort the findings.

The use of models is another key component of statistical thinking. Models are simplified representations of complex realities, constructed to capture essential relationships and to make predictions. In statistics, models are often built using assumptions about the distribution of data, the nature of relationships between variables, and the mechanisms generating the data. These models are not judged solely on how well they fit the data but also on how well they generalize to new data. This distinction between fitting and generalizing lies at the core of the bias-variance tradeoff, a fundamental concept in both traditional statistics and modern machine learning.

A statistical thinker is also deeply concerned with the concept of inference. Inference refers to the process of drawing conclusions about a population based on a sample. It involves estimating parameters, testing hypotheses, and quantifying uncertainty. Importantly, inference is not about proving a result to be definitively true or false, but rather about assessing how strongly the data supports one conclusion over another. This probabilistic approach to reasoning stands in contrast to deterministic thinking and allows for more nuanced decision-making. Confidence intervals, p-values, and posterior probabilities are all tools that emerge from this inferential mindset, each offering a way to quantify our beliefs in light of the evidence.

Moreover, statistical thinking encourages skepticism and critical analysis. It trains data scientists to question assumptions, evaluate methodologies, and consider alternative explanations. No statistical analysis exists in a vacuum; every model is built on assumptions, and every result is contingent on the data and methods used. A statistically literate person is aware of the limitations of their analysis and communicates these limitations transparently. This humility is essential in a field where decisions can have significant consequences, from public policy to healthcare and beyond.

Finally, the foundations of statistical thought are inseparable from ethics. The way data is collected, analyzed, and presented carries ethical implications. Statistical thinking promotes honesty, transparency, and reproducibility. It urges practitioners to avoid manipulating results to fit a narrative and to be vigilant against misleading visualizations or selective reporting. Ethical statistical practice demands that uncertainty is acknowledged, not hidden, and that the rights and privacy of data subjects are respected.

In sum, statistical thinking is not merely a collection of formulas and techniques but a disciplined way of approaching problems in the presence of uncertainty. It blends mathematical rigor with philosophical depth, encouraging data scientists to be precise, cautious, and reflective in their work. As data continues to grow in volume and complexity, the principles of statistical thought remain as crucial as ever, forming the intellectual foundation upon which responsible and insightful data science is built.

The Role of Uncertainty in Data Science

Uncertainty is a fundamental aspect of data science, shaping how data is interpreted, how models are built, and how decisions are made. In a world overflowing with information, it is tempting to believe that data holds absolute truths waiting to be uncovered. However, data is rarely complete, measurements are often noisy, and the processes generating data are frequently complex and only partially understood. Recognizing and accounting for uncertainty is not a limitation but a strength of data science. It reflects a mature and honest approach to the limits of knowledge, enabling practitioners to produce more robust, reliable, and ethical analyses.

At the heart of statistical reasoning is the understanding that uncertainty is intrinsic to every dataset. Whether it arises from sampling variability, measurement error, or model imperfections, uncertainty is ever-present. For instance, when a company surveys a thousand customers to gauge satisfaction, their findings are only an estimate of the sentiment of the entire customer base. Different samples might yield slightly different results due to randomness. This variation is not a flaw but a natural outcome of working with samples. Statistical tools exist to quantify this variation, allowing analysts to express how confident they are in their estimates.

Probability theory provides the mathematical language through which uncertainty is articulated. Rather than giving a single deterministic answer, a probability-based approach offers a range of possible outcomes, each with an associated likelihood. This probabilistic mindset allows data scientists to model the unknown not as a binary question of true or false, but as a spectrum of possibilities. When estimating a parameter, for example, one can provide a confidence interval, indicating a range in which the true value likely falls. When making predictions, one can describe not just the expected outcome but also the spread and shape of possible outcomes.

Decision-making under uncertainty is a central challenge in data science. Organizations must often act based on incomplete information, choosing strategies that carry risks and trade-offs. Statistical models help evaluate these risks by simulating potential scenarios and assessing their consequences. For instance, in clinical trials, researchers do not claim with certainty that a treatment works; instead, they report the probability that observed benefits could have occurred by chance. This nuanced perspective allows for more informed decisions, balancing the potential for gain against the risk of error. It is not about eliminating uncertainty but about managing it intelligently.

One important source of uncertainty in data science is sampling variability. When drawing conclusions about a population from a sample, the results are subject to chance. Even with random sampling, different samples produce different estimates. This sampling error is inevitable but quantifiable. Through techniques such as bootstrapping and the use of standard errors, data scientists can evaluate the stability of their results. Confidence intervals derived from this analysis help stakeholders understand the precision of estimates and avoid overinterpreting point values that are, in reality, just one of many plausible outcomes.

Another key aspect of uncertainty comes from the process of measurement. Real-world data collection is often messy. Sensors may drift, humans may make errors in recording data, and definitions may shift over time. Even when precision is high, there is always a layer of noise in any empirical measurement. Ignoring this uncertainty can lead to overconfidence in results, potentially leading to flawed conclusions or misguided actions. Statistical models incorporate error terms to account for this noise, ensuring that interpretations remain grounded in reality. A model that does not acknowledge measurement error is likely to mislead, especially when used for forecasting or decision support.

Modeling uncertainty is not only about acknowledging errors in measurement or sampling but also about the limits of the models themselves. All models are simplifications, built on assumptions that may or may not hold in the real world. Linear models assume a constant rate of change; classification models assume that patterns observed in training data generalize to new situations. These assumptions introduce uncertainty because real systems are rarely so tidy. Bayesian methods offer one approach to incorporate uncertainty about model parameters explicitly, using prior beliefs updated with new data to produce a posterior distribution. This approach reflects the reality that knowledge evolves with evidence and that confidence should grow or shrink depending on what the data reveals.

Uncertainty also plays a crucial role in evaluating model performance. Predictive models do not guarantee perfect accuracy. Instead, they produce outputs that reflect probabilities. A classification model might predict that a customer has a 70 percent chance of churning. Whether the customer ultimately churns or not does not invalidate the model; what matters is whether the model performs well across many cases. Calibration plots, confidence intervals, and probabilistic scoring rules are all tools used to evaluate whether a model is properly representing uncertainty. Overconfident models, which assign high probabilities to outcomes that rarely occur, are dangerous and misleading.

The communication of uncertainty is a critical responsibility for data scientists. It is not enough to produce rigorous analyses; findings must be presented in ways that convey the inherent uncertainty without causing confusion or distrust. This requires skillful storytelling, visualizations that include confidence bands or error bars, and language that avoids unwarranted certainty. Decision-makers rely on data scientists not just for numbers, but for insight into how much trust to place in those numbers. Being transparent about what is known, what is estimated, and what is unknown builds credibility and helps prevent costly mistakes based on overconfident interpretations.

Moreover, ethical data science depends on a clear understanding of uncertainty. Decisions made under the illusion of certainty can lead to unjust or harmful outcomes. For example, predictive policing models that do not account for uncertainty in crime data may perpetuate biases and reinforce existing inequalities. In healthcare, overreliance on predictive scores without understanding their uncertainty can result in improper diagnoses or treatment plans. Recognizing uncertainty fosters humility, encourages careful validation, and promotes more equitable outcomes. It ensures that models are not treated as oracles but as tools, fallible and in need of constant scrutiny.

In every phase of the data science process—from data collection and exploration to modeling, interpretation, and decision-making—uncertainty is a companion. It cannot be eliminated, but it can be understood, measured, and managed. Embracing uncertainty does not weaken the power of data science; rather, it strengthens it by acknowledging complexity and guarding against false precision. This mindset elevates the practice of data science from mere calculation to thoughtful, informed reasoning in the face of the unknown.

Probability Basics for Data Analysis

Probability serves as the foundational language of uncertainty in data analysis. Without a firm grasp of probability, it becomes difficult to make sense of randomness, variation, and the countless sources of noise that permeate real-world data. In data science, probability is not an abstract mathematical concept but a practical framework that allows analysts to quantify what they know, estimate what they do not, and evaluate the likelihood of different outcomes. It is the tool that bridges the gap between observed data and the conclusions we can draw from them. A deep understanding of probability enables data scientists to make rational predictions, assess risks, and build models that can navigate the complexity and uncertainty inherent in empirical data.

At its core, probability provides a structured way to think about chance. It allows us to assign numerical values between zero and one to the likelihood of events occurring, where zero means an event is impossible and one indicates certainty. These values obey a set of formal rules, such as the requirement that the total probability of all mutually exclusive outcomes in a given context must sum to one. These foundational rules make probability a consistent and logical system for reasoning about uncertain phenomena. Whether one is analyzing medical data, evaluating marketing outcomes, or modeling stock market behavior, probability forms the underpinning logic of the entire analytical process.

In practical terms, data scientists often begin by working with discrete probability models. These models describe systems with a countable number of possible outcomes. For instance, consider a data analysis scenario involving customer churn. A customer either remains or leaves, and we can model this binary outcome using a simple discrete distribution. More complex situations might involve multiple categories or repeated trials, such as the number of times a user clicks on a webpage out of several visits. In such cases, discrete probability distributions like the binomial or Poisson become essential tools. Each provides formulas for computing the likelihood of different outcomes under specific conditions, helping analysts understand how unusual or expected their data might be.

As data becomes more detailed and continuous in nature, continuous probability distributions come into play. These distributions are used when the variable of interest can take on any value within a range, such as height, weight, or temperature. The normal distribution, with its bell-shaped curve, is perhaps the most well-known of these. It arises naturally in many contexts due to the central limit theorem, which states that the sum or average of many small, independent random variables tends to be normally distributed, regardless of their original distribution. This principle is foundational for many inferential methods, allowing data scientists to use the normal distribution as an approximation in a wide variety of settings.

Probability also plays a central role in the concept of conditional probability, which refers to the probability of one event occurring given that another has occurred. This is especially relevant in data analysis, where relationships between variables are often conditional rather than absolute. For example, the probability that a customer makes a purchase might depend on whether they received a promotional email. Understanding these dependencies allows analysts to build more accurate predictive models and to uncover patterns that would remain hidden if variables were considered in isolation. Conditional probability is also the basis for Bayes' theorem, a powerful result that allows for the updating of beliefs in light of new evidence, and which underlies many Bayesian approaches to data science.

Joint and marginal probabilities further expand the analyst's ability to reason about complex data structures. Joint probability deals with the likelihood of multiple events occurring together, while marginal probability considers the likelihood of a single event regardless of other variables. These concepts become particularly useful when working with multidimensional datasets, where outcomes may be influenced by a combination of factors. By understanding how to decompose and reconstruct probabilities in such scenarios, data scientists can better analyze patterns, test hypotheses, and build more informative models.

Probability also informs the idea of independence, a critical assumption in many statistical methods. Two events are said to be independent if the occurrence of one does not affect the probability of the other. In data analysis, this assumption often simplifies calculations and model building, but it must be treated with caution. Real-world data rarely behaves in fully independent ways, and failing to account for dependencies can lead to misleading results. Careful probability reasoning helps analysts test for independence and to adjust their methods when dependencies are present.

The application of probability extends beyond theory into practical techniques such as simulation and probabilistic modeling. When analytical solutions are difficult or impossible to obtain, simulation offers a way to approximate probabilities through repeated random sampling. Monte Carlo methods, for instance, rely on random draws to estimate probabilities and outcomes in complex systems. These approaches are widely used in risk analysis, optimization, and machine learning, where they allow for flexible modeling of uncertainty and complex interactions between variables.

In the realm of machine learning, probability is also a core component of many algorithms. Naive Bayes classifiers use conditional probabilities to categorize data based on features. Probabilistic graphical models like Bayesian networks represent dependencies among variables in a structured way. Even deep learning models can be understood in probabilistic terms, especially when uncertainty estimation and confidence intervals are needed for predictions. The probabilistic interpretation of these models enhances their transparency and provides critical information for decision-making.

Overall, probability equips data scientists with the language and tools necessary to handle uncertainty rigorously. It provides a way to formalize intuition about chance, to evaluate the plausibility of hypotheses, and to quantify confidence in results. Whether analyzing a single dataset or building complex predictive models, probability serves as the silent engine driving the entire process. Through probability, data analysis transforms from mere observation into a disciplined approach to learning from data, one that acknowledges the limits of knowledge while striving to push those limits forward with each new insight.

Random Variables and Distributions

Random variables and their associated probability distributions are central to the mathematical structure that underpins statistical reasoning and data science. These concepts allow us to model uncertainty in a formal and interpretable way, transforming raw randomness into analyzable data. A random variable is a numerical representation of the outcomes of a random process. It assigns values to each possible outcome of a probabilistic event, thereby turning abstract randomness into something quantifiable. By defining a random variable, data scientists create a bridge between the real-world phenomena they study and the statistical models they use to understand and predict those phenomena.

There are two main types of random variables: discrete and continuous. A discrete random variable takes on a countable number of possible values. This could include things like the number of customers who visit a store on a given day, the number of heads in a series of coin tosses, or the number of times a web page is refreshed. Each value of a discrete random variable is associated with a probability, and the collection of these values and their probabilities forms what is known as a probability mass function. This function tells us how likely it is to observe each possible outcome. For instance, in a binomial experiment where a coin is flipped ten times, the probability mass function can tell us how likely it is to get exactly five heads.

In contrast, a continuous random variable can take on an infinite number of values within a given range. Common examples include the height of individuals, the temperature in a city, or the time it takes for a webpage to load. Since there are infinitely many possible values in any interval, the probability of the variable taking on any one specific value is technically zero. Instead, probabilities are assigned over intervals. The mathematical tool used here is the probability density function, which describes the relative likelihood of the variable falling within a particular range. The area under the curve of this function over a given interval represents the probability that the variable falls within that interval.

Understanding the behavior of random variables involves exploring their distributions. A distribution describes how the values of a random variable are spread out, which values are more likely, and which are less likely. This idea captures not just central tendencies but also the spread, shape, and tail behavior of the variable. For example, the normal distribution, which is symmetrical and bell-shaped, models many natural phenomena due to the central limit theorem. It is used extensively in statistical inference because it approximates the behavior of averages of large numbers of random variables, regardless of their original distributions.

Other important distributions include the binomial, which models the number of successes in a fixed number of independent Bernoulli trials; the Poisson, which models the number of events occurring in a fixed interval of time or space when these events occur independently; and the exponential, which describes the time between successive events in a Poisson process. Each of these distributions has a specific structure and set of parameters that determine its shape and behavior. By selecting the appropriate distribution, data scientists can model real-world processes with precision and use those models to generate predictions, conduct tests, or inform decision-making.

Every distribution has certain characteristics that help describe and summarize it. The most basic of these are the mean and variance. The mean of a random variable gives its expected value, a measure of its central tendency, while the variance quantifies the spread of its values around the mean. Higher moments such as skewness and kurtosis describe the asymmetry and the heaviness of the tails of the distribution, respectively. These properties give a more detailed picture of the distribution's shape and are important in selecting suitable models and in understanding how extreme values might influence outcomes.

The cumulative distribution function is another fundamental concept. For any given value of a random variable, the cumulative distribution function gives the probability that the variable takes on a value less than or equal to that point. This function is useful for computing probabilities over ranges and for understanding the overall behavior of the distribution. It plays a central role in hypothesis testing, model comparison, and generating random samples for simulation.

One of the most powerful aspects of working with random variables and distributions is the ability to simulate complex systems. Through random number generation and transformation methods, data scientists can create artificial datasets that follow a specific distribution. These simulations are useful for evaluating statistical procedures, modeling scenarios that are difficult to observe directly, and estimating probabilities or other quantities that are analytically intractable. Monte Carlo methods, for instance, rely heavily on repeated sampling from probability distributions to approximate solutions to complex problems in physics, finance, and machine learning.

Joint distributions extend the idea of random variables to multivariate settings, where two or more variables are considered simultaneously. In many real-world problems, outcomes are not independent, and the relationship between random variables must be captured through their joint behavior. The joint distribution specifies the probability of different combinations of outcomes occurring together. From the joint distribution, marginal distributions and conditional distributions can be derived, allowing analysts to study the individual behavior of variables and how one variable may influence another. These relationships are central to understanding correlation, causation, and dependence structures in data.

Transformations of random variables are also an important area in probability theory. When a random variable undergoes a transformation, such as squaring or taking the logarithm, its distribution changes. Understanding how the distribution changes under transformation is essential for data preprocessing, normalization, and the development of certain statistical models. Sometimes, transformations are used to make data more compatible with model assumptions or to achieve linearity in regression analysis.

Random variables and distributions thus form the mathematical infrastructure of probabilistic thinking in data science. They allow uncertainty to be expressed precisely, guide the formulation of hypotheses, and support the development of models that can adapt to real-world complexities. By mastering these concepts, data scientists equip themselves with the tools necessary to turn data into insight, to distinguish meaningful patterns from random noise, and to support decisions with a clear understanding of the risks and variability involved.

Expectation, Variance, and Covariance

Expectation, variance, and covariance are three essential concepts in probability and statistics that provide a deeper understanding of random variables and their behavior. These mathematical tools allow data scientists to summarize, compare, and interpret distributions in meaningful ways. While raw data can provide insight on its own, it is through the lens of these measures that patterns become clearer, variability is quantified, and relationships between variables are revealed. Each concept offers a different perspective: expectation focuses on central tendency, variance captures the spread of data, and covariance assesses how two variables move in relation to one another. Together, they form the bedrock of much of modern statistical modeling and inference.

The expectation, also known as the expected value or mean, is a measure of the central location of a random variable. It represents the long-run average value of the variable if the random process were repeated infinitely many times. Mathematically, for a discrete random variable, the expectation is calculated by summing the products of each possible value and its associated probability. For continuous random variables, the expectation is computed as the integral of the product of the variable's value and its probability density function over the entire range of values. Expectation gives a concise summary of where a distribution is centered. In practical terms, it tells us what value to expect on average, even if that value might not actually be observed in any specific instance.

Expectation is also a linear operator, which means it satisfies certain useful mathematical properties. For example, the expected value of the sum of two random variables is the sum of their expected values. This property makes expectation a powerful tool in data analysis and probabilistic modeling. It allows analysts to decompose complex expressions and estimate averages of composite functions. In risk management, for instance, the expected value of a financial portfolio can be assessed by computing the weighted average of expected returns across different assets. This simple yet profound concept lies at the heart of decision theory, economics, and statistical estimation.

Variance, on the other hand, quantifies how much the values of a random variable deviate from their expected value. It is defined as the expected value of the squared deviation from the mean. In other words, it measures the average of the squares of the differences between observed values and the mean of the distribution. A high variance indicates that the values of the variable are spread out over a wide range, while a low variance implies that they cluster closely around the mean. Variance is essential for understanding the stability or volatility of a random process. In financial modeling, for example, variance is used to assess the risk associated with different investments. A higher variance suggests a higher level of uncertainty or potential for deviation from expected returns.

Because variance involves squaring the deviations, its units are not in the same scale as the original variable. For this reason, the standard deviation, which is the square root of the variance, is often used in practical applications. The standard deviation returns the measure of spread to the same scale as the original data, making it easier to interpret. Still, variance remains a critical component in many statistical procedures, including hypothesis testing, analysis of variance (ANOVA), and regression analysis. It is also a building block in more advanced techniques such as principal component analysis, which seeks to reduce the dimensionality of data while preserving variance as much as possible.

Covariance extends the idea of variance to pairs of random variables. While variance measures how a single variable deviates from its mean, covariance measures how two variables vary together. If two variables tend to increase or decrease together, their covariance is positive. If one tends to increase while the other decreases, the covariance is negative. A covariance near zero suggests that there is little to no linear relationship between the variables. Covariance is computed as the expected value of the product of the deviations of each variable from their respective means. This value gives insight into the direction of the relationship between variables but not its strength or consistency.

The interpretation of covariance is often made clearer through normalization. Dividing the covariance by the product of the standard deviations of the two variables yields the correlation coefficient, which is a standardized measure ranging between -1 and 1. This coefficient provides a clearer picture of the strength and direction of a linear relationship, independent of the units of the variables. Nonetheless, covariance itself remains a crucial component in many multivariate techniques. It appears in the construction of covariance matrices, which are used to understand the joint variability of multiple variables. Covariance matrices are fundamental to multivariate statistics, serving as the foundation for methods like multivariate normal distributions, Mahalanobis distance, and factor analysis.

In machine learning and statistical modeling, understanding covariance is vital for selecting features and constructing predictive models. If two features are highly correlated, they may convey redundant information. This redundancy can affect the performance and interpretability of models, especially in regression and classification tasks. By analyzing the covariance structure of the data, practitioners can identify which variables provide unique and useful information and which ones might be contributing to multicollinearity or overfitting.

Moreover, expectation, variance, and covariance are not just theoretical constructs. They have tangible implications in real-world data science problems. When building simulations, computing estimators, or constructing probabilistic models, these measures guide the choice of algorithms and evaluation criteria. They are used to compare models, estimate errors, and quantify uncertainty. Even in black-box models like neural networks, techniques such as dropout and regularization implicitly aim to control variance to avoid overfitting.

These three concepts form the mathematical language for describing and analyzing randomness. They enable the construction of more robust models, more accurate predictions, and more reliable inferences. A strong grasp of expectation, variance, and covariance equips data scientists with the tools to dissect data, identify patterns, and make decisions grounded in statistical reasoning. Whether one is dealing with a simple linear regression or a complex probabilistic graphical model, these foundational ideas remain central to the entire enterprise of data analysis.

The Law of Large Numbers

The Law of Large Numbers is one of the most fundamental and profound theorems in probability theory, serving as a cornerstone of statistical reasoning and a guiding principle in data science. It formalizes the intuitive idea that as the size of a sample increases, the average of the sample values tends to get closer to the expected value of the population from which the sample is drawn. This law is not just a mathematical curiosity; it is a powerful guarantee that supports the reliability of empirical averages, giving data scientists the confidence to use samples to infer properties of much larger populations.

At the heart of the Law of Large Numbers is the concept of stability through repetition. When we observe a random process a few times, the results can fluctuate wildly. But as we increase the number of observations, the irregularities begin to cancel each other out, and the average result begins to stabilize. This is the key insight: randomness produces noise in the short run, but order emerges in the long run. In a world filled with uncertainty, the Law of Large Numbers provides the foundation for extracting meaningful insights from data.

There are two main versions of this law: the weak law and the strong law. Both express the same essential idea, but in slightly different ways. The weak law states that for a sequence of independent and identically distributed random variables with a finite expected value, the sample average converges in probability to the expected value as the sample size approaches infinity. This means that the probability that the sample average deviates from the true mean by more than a small amount becomes arbitrarily small as the number of observations grows. The strong law goes a step further by stating that this convergence happens almost surely, or with probability one. That is, the sample average converges to the expected value for nearly every possible sequence of outcomes. While the technical distinctions between the two versions are subtle, both confirm that with enough data, randomness becomes predictable in a statistical sense.

The implications of the Law of Large Numbers are vast. In practice, it allows researchers and analysts to rely on sample statistics as proxies for population parameters. Whether estimating the average income in a city, the mean temperature over a decade, or the defect rate in a manufacturing process, the law reassures us that these sample estimates are not arbitrary. Instead, they are grounded in a powerful probabilistic guarantee that they will approximate the true values closely, provided the sample size is sufficiently large.

This principle also helps explain why small samples can be misleading. When working with limited data, random variation can dominate, leading to results that are far from the population truth. This is why polls and surveys often report margins of error and confidence levels, which reflect the degree of uncertainty due to sample size. In many real-world applications, small sample sizes have led to incorrect inferences, spurious correlations, or overconfident predictions. The Law of Large Numbers reminds us that statistical reliability grows with the number of observations, and that caution must be exercised when working with small datasets.

In the field of machine learning, the Law of Large Numbers plays a crucial role in the training of models. Many learning algorithms rely on empirical averages to estimate gradients, update parameters, and evaluate performance. The stability and convergence of these estimates depend on having enough data. As the training dataset grows, the estimates become more accurate, reducing the variance of the model and improving generalization to unseen data. Overfitting becomes less of a concern, and the model's performance metrics become more trustworthy. In this way, the law underpins the common wisdom in data science that more data leads to better models.

Simulation studies also rely heavily on the Law of Large Numbers. In many complex systems, exact analytical solutions are not feasible, and simulation becomes the primary tool for estimation. By running simulations thousands or millions of times and averaging the outcomes, data scientists can approximate expected values, probabilities, and other quantities of interest with increasing precision. Monte Carlo methods, for example, are entirely based on this principle. The accuracy of the results depends on the number of simulated trials, and the Law of Large Numbers guarantees that these results converge to the true values as the number of trials increases.

The law also informs the design of experiments and observational studies. When determining sample sizes, researchers use the Law of Large Numbers to calculate how many observations are needed to achieve a desired level of precision. This allows them to balance the costs of data collection with the benefits of statistical accuracy. The law provides a mathematical justification for investing in larger datasets, especially when decisions or policies depend on the accuracy of the estimates derived from those datasets.

Moreover, the Law of Large Numbers has philosophical implications for how we understand probability and randomness. It shows that while individual events are unpredictable, aggregate patterns are not. This shift from unpredictability to predictability through aggregation is a central theme in statistics. It allows scientists to make meaningful statements about populations, even when individual behavior remains uncertain. This is particularly important in fields like epidemiology, economics, and social science, where individual variability is high, but collective behavior exhibits regularity.

Despite its power, the Law of Large Numbers should not be misunderstood as a guarantee that any given large sample will yield an accurate result. It operates in the limit, meaning that convergence to the expected value is only assured as the sample size becomes very large. There is no fixed number of observations after which the average becomes exact. The speed of convergence can depend on the underlying distribution, the presence of outliers, and the variability of the data. Heavy-tailed distributions, for instance, may require much larger samples to observe stable averages due to the influence of extreme values. Understanding these nuances helps avoid overconfidence and reinforces the importance of proper data analysis.

In summary, the Law of Large Numbers provides the theoretical assurance that sampling and statistical estimation are reliable strategies for learning from data. It transforms randomness into stability and forms the basis for everything from polling to model training to scientific discovery. By grasping this concept, data scientists gain the ability to navigate uncertainty with mathematical confidence and to build systems that grow more accurate and dependable as they are fed with more data.

The Central Limit Theorem

The Central Limit Theorem is one of the most powerful and widely used results in all of statistics and probability. It provides the mathematical foundation for making inferences about populations based on sample data, regardless of the original distribution of the population. This remarkable theorem reveals that under fairly general conditions, the distribution of the sum or average of a large number of independent and identically distributed random variables tends toward a normal distribution, even if the original variables themselves are not normally distributed. In practical terms, this means that many real-world phenomena, which may be inherently non-normal, can still be analyzed using tools derived from the normal distribution, provided that we are working with large enough samples.

The Central Limit Theorem is not only elegant in its theoretical formulation but also profoundly useful in application. In data science, it justifies the use of normal approximation in countless procedures, including the construction of confidence intervals, hypothesis testing, and the evaluation of statistical estimators. It bridges the gap between the often messy, irregular world of raw data and the orderly, mathematically tractable world of the normal distribution. This bridge allows practitioners to apply consistent and reliable methods even in situations where the underlying data may be skewed, heavy-tailed, or otherwise non-Gaussian.

The core idea of the Central Limit Theorem can be described as follows. Suppose we take repeated samples from a population with a finite mean and variance. For each sample, we compute the sample mean. If we repeat this process a large number of times, generating a distribution of sample means, that distribution will approximate a normal distribution as the sample size increases. This result holds true regardless of the shape of the population distribution, provided that the samples are independent and identically distributed and that the population variance is finite. This universality is what gives the theorem its immense power and utility.

One of the most striking aspects of the Central Limit Theorem is that it applies to a wide range of distributions. Whether the original data come from a uniform, exponential, binomial, or even a highly skewed distribution, the distribution of the sample mean will still converge to normality as the sample size grows. This property explains why the normal distribution appears so frequently in statistics and in the natural and social sciences. It is not necessarily because the phenomena themselves are normally distributed, but because the process of aggregation through averaging leads to a normal-like behavior.

The rate at which this convergence occurs depends on the characteristics of the original distribution. For distributions that are already close to normal, convergence happens rapidly, even with small sample sizes. For distributions with heavy tails or significant skewness, larger sample sizes are needed to achieve a good approximation. Nonetheless, the theorem assures us that the approximation will improve with more data. In practical settings, it is often observed that even with samples as small as thirty, the sample mean is approximately normally distributed. This rule of thumb allows analysts to begin applying normal-based methods with relatively modest data requirements.

In inferential statistics, the Central Limit Theorem underlies the rationale for constructing confidence intervals and conducting significance tests. When we use a sample mean to estimate a population mean, we are relying on the fact that the distribution of the sample mean is normal or approximately normal, which allows us to make probability-based statements about the accuracy of our estimate. For instance, we can calculate a 95 percent confidence interval around the sample mean, indicating the range within which the true population mean is likely to fall. Without the Central Limit Theorem, such calculations would be difficult or impossible for non-normal populations.

The theorem is also essential in the evaluation of the sampling distribution of other statistics. While it is most commonly associated with the sample mean, it also applies to sums and, in certain conditions, to more complex functions of random variables. The generality of the Central Limit Theorem means that it can be adapted to various settings, including stratified sampling, bootstrapping methods, and linear combinations of variables. In regression analysis, for example, the sampling distribution of the estimated coefficients can be approximated using the Central Limit Theorem, which in turn allows for hypothesis testing and the construction of confidence intervals around those coefficients.

Another important application of the Central Limit Theorem is in quality control and industrial statistics. In manufacturing processes, where consistency is key, analysts often rely on control charts to monitor variation. These charts are built on the assumption that the sampling distribution of the process mean is normal. The Central Limit Theorem provides the theoretical justification for this assumption, ensuring that quality assessments and decisions based on these charts are statistically sound.

In machine learning and artificial intelligence, the theorem plays a supporting role in the development and evaluation of algorithms. Many algorithms involve stochastic processes, random initialization, or sampling from distributions. Understanding the probabilistic behavior of these elements often relies on the principles of the Central Limit Theorem. For instance, when performing cross-validation or ensemble modeling, the aggregation of multiple models or predictions can be better understood and improved through the lens of the theorem. The reliability and stability of ensemble predictions increase as more models are aggregated, reflecting the same convergence behavior described by the theorem.

Even in simulation and Monte Carlo methods, the Central Limit Theorem remains indispensable. When approximating expectations or probabilities through repeated random sampling, the accuracy of these estimates improves with the number of samples, and the distribution of the sample means becomes increasingly normal. This convergence allows practitioners to assess the error of their estimates and to construct confidence intervals, even when the underlying simulations are based on complex and unknown distributions.

The Central Limit Theorem is more than a theoretical result; it is a practical guide for navigating uncertainty and for making sound statistical decisions in the face of incomplete or irregular data. Its assurances allow data scientists to proceed with confidence, knowing that their tools are grounded in a principle that brings structure to randomness. Whether estimating parameters, building models, validating hypotheses, or simulating outcomes, the Central Limit Theorem stands as a silent yet powerful ally in the quest to understand the patterns hidden within data.

Populations and Samples

In the practice of statistics and data science, the distinction between populations and samples lies at the heart of almost every analytical process. These two concepts are foundational, forming the conceptual framework that allows analysts to draw conclusions about vast groups of interest using only a subset of data. A population refers to the entire set of items, individuals, or events that a study aims to understand or describe. It is the complete universe of potential observations, which may be finite, such as all registered voters in a country, or effectively infinite, such as all future customers of a product. A sample, by contrast, is a smaller, manageable subset of that population, selected for the purpose of study. It is through samples that we attempt to infer properties of the population, using statistical techniques to bridge the gap between the part we can observe and the whole that we cannot.

The necessity of sampling arises from the practical limitations of time, cost, and accessibility. In most real-world scenarios, it is simply not feasible to collect data from an entire population. Measuring the cholesterol levels of every adult in a country, or monitoring every machine in a global supply chain, would be prohibitively expensive and logistically impossible. Sampling allows researchers to obtain a snapshot of the population's characteristics using a relatively small number of observations. However, the validity of any conclusion drawn from a sample depends heavily on how the sample is chosen and how representative it is of the population as a whole. This makes the design and selection of samples a critical step in any statistical investigation.

Random sampling is one of the most important tools for ensuring that a sample accurately reflects the population. In a simple random sample, every member of the population has an equal chance of being selected. This minimizes selection bias and increases the likelihood that the sample will be representative. Other sampling methods, such as stratified sampling, cluster sampling, or systematic sampling, may be used depending on the structure of the population and the goals of the analysis. Each method has strengths and limitations, and choosing the appropriate one requires a clear understanding of the context and the questions being asked.

Once a sample is collected, analysts use it to estimate population parameters. Parameters are numerical values that describe characteristics of the population, such as the population mean, variance, or proportion. Because the population is usually not fully observable, these parameters are unknown. Instead, we compute statistics from the sample, such as the sample mean or sample standard deviation, which serve as estimates of the corresponding parameters. These estimates are subject to sampling variability, meaning that different samples from the same population will yield slightly different results. This inherent variability is quantified through concepts such as standard errors, confidence intervals, and hypothesis testing, all of which rely on the mathematical properties of samples and their distributions.

Understanding the relationship between a sample and its population also involves acknowledging the possibility of bias and error. Sampling bias occurs when some members of the population are systematically more likely to be included in the sample than others. This can lead to distorted estimates and flawed conclusions. For example, if a survey about healthcare is conducted only online, it may miss older individuals who are less likely to use the internet, thus underrepresenting a significant segment of the population. Nonresponse bias, measurement error, and coverage error are additional threats to the validity of inferences drawn from samples. Recognizing and mitigating these issues is a vital part of responsible data analysis.

The size of the sample is another factor that strongly influences the reliability of estimates. Larger samples tend to produce more accurate and stable estimates of population parameters because they reduce the impact of random variation. The Law of Large Numbers assures us that as the sample size increases, the sample mean will converge to the population mean. However, collecting large samples can be expensive or time-consuming, so data scientists must balance the benefits of increased precision against the costs of data collection. Determining the optimal sample size involves considerations of statistical power, confidence level, and the acceptable margin of error.

In experimental design, distinguishing between the population and the sample is equally critical. When testing a new treatment or intervention, the goal is to make claims about how it would work in the general population. The individuals who participate in the trial form a sample, and the results observed from this group are generalized to a broader population. Ensuring that this sample is diverse and representative is key to making valid conclusions. Randomization, blinding, and control groups are tools that help maintain the integrity of the sample and support valid inferences.

Data science also deals with big data, where the amount of data collected can be so large that it resembles a population in itself. Yet even in such scenarios, the data may not represent the full population of interest. For instance, analyzing social media data may involve billions of records, but those records still represent only people who use those platforms. The challenge, then, is not just about sample size but about representativeness. A massive, non-representative sample may yield misleading insights, while a smaller, well-constructed sample may provide more accurate and generalizable results.

Populations and samples also play a central role in predictive modeling. When training a model, the training data constitutes a sample from a broader data-generating process. The goal is to build a model that performs well not just on the training data but also on new, unseen data from the same population. Overfitting occurs when a model learns the noise and idiosyncrasies of the sample rather than the underlying patterns in the population. Cross-validation, regularization, and careful feature selection are among the strategies used to ensure that models generalize beyond the sample on which they were trained.

The interplay between populations and samples underlies every aspect of statistical inference and machine learning. It governs how we collect data, how we interpret it, and how we transform data into actionable knowledge. A deep understanding of these concepts is essential for anyone working with data, as it ensures that conclusions are not only statistically sound but also practically relevant. Through rigorous sampling, thoughtful analysis, and a clear appreciation of the limits of data, data scientists can extract insights that truly reflect the world they aim to understand.

Sampling Distributions and Estimators

Sampling distributions and estimators are fundamental concepts in statistical inference, forming the bridge between raw sample data and broader population-level conclusions. They provide the mathematical framework through which data scientists can quantify uncertainty, evaluate the reliability of their estimates, and make informed decisions based on partial information. A sampling distribution refers to the probability distribution of a given statistic, such as the sample mean or sample variance, over all possible samples of a fixed size drawn from a population. An estimator, on the other hand, is a rule or formula that provides an estimate of a population parameter based on sample data. Together, these ideas form the core of statistical estimation and help define how confident we can be in our conclusions drawn from limited data.

When we draw a sample from a population and compute a statistic, we are performing a single instance of a process that could be repeated many times. If we were to repeat the sampling process again and again, each time taking a new random sample of the same size and computing the same statistic, the values of the statistic would vary from sample to sample. This variability gives rise to the sampling distribution of the statistic. For example, if we repeatedly sample from a population and compute the sample mean each time, the distribution of those sample means across all possible samples forms the sampling distribution of the mean. Understanding this distribution allows us to assess the reliability of the sample mean as an estimate of the true population mean.

The shape and properties of a sampling distribution depend on several factors, including the population distribution, the sample size, and the estimator being used. One of the most important results in statistics is that, under certain conditions, the sampling distribution of the sample mean becomes approximately normal as the sample size increases, regardless of the shape of the population distribution. This result is guaranteed by the Central Limit Theorem and is critical because it justifies the use of normal-based inference methods even when the population itself is not normally distributed. For sufficiently large sample sizes, the sample mean follows a normal distribution centered around the population mean, with a standard deviation known as the standard error.

The standard error measures the spread of the sampling distribution and quantifies how much variability we can expect in our estimator from sample to sample. It is influenced by the sample size and the variability of the population. Specifically, for the sample mean, the standard error is equal to the population standard deviation divided by the square root of the sample size. As the sample size increases, the standard error decreases, indicating that larger samples tend to yield more precise estimates. This inverse relationship between sample size and standard error emphasizes the value of large, representative samples in statistical analysis.

Estimators themselves can be evaluated according to several key properties, which help determine their quality and usefulness. One of the most important properties is unbiasedness. An estimator is said to be unbiased if its expected value is equal to the true value of the population parameter. In other words, on average, the estimator hits the target. For instance, the sample mean is an unbiased estimator of the population mean. Another desirable property is consistency, which means that as the sample size grows, the estimator converges to the true parameter value. A consistent estimator becomes increasingly accurate as more data becomes available, reinforcing the idea that larger samples provide better estimates.

Efficiency is another important criterion for comparing estimators. Among a set of unbiased estimators, the one with the smallest variance is considered the most efficient because it tends to produce estimates that are closer to the true parameter. The efficiency of an estimator affects the precision of statistical inference, influencing the width of confidence intervals and the power of hypothesis tests. In practice, data scientists often face trade-offs among these properties. For example, an estimator might be unbiased but have high variance, or it might be slightly biased but exhibit much lower variability, making it more reliable in finite samples.

Another critical concept related to estimators and sampling distributions is the idea of sufficiency. A sufficient estimator captures all the information in the data relevant to the parameter being estimated. If an estimator is sufficient, no other statistic derived from the same sample provides additional information about the parameter. The concept of sufficiency plays a key role in the development of optimal estimation procedures and in the construction of likelihood-based inference methods.

The sampling distribution is not only essential for estimation but also forms the basis for statistical testing and the construction of confidence intervals. When conducting a hypothesis test, we compare the observed value of a test statistic to its sampling distribution under the null hypothesis. This allows us to calculate p-values and determine whether the observed result is statistically significant. Similarly, confidence intervals are constructed using the sampling distribution of an estimator. A confidence interval provides a range of values within which the true parameter is likely to fall, given the observed data. The width of the interval depends on the standard error and the desired level of confidence.

Simulation methods such as bootstrapping provide a flexible approach to approximating sampling distributions when analytical solutions are difficult or unavailable. Bootstrapping involves repeatedly resampling the observed data with replacement and recalculating the statistic of interest for each resample. This generates an empirical approximation of the sampling distribution, which can then be used to estimate standard errors, construct confidence intervals, or perform hypothesis tests. The appeal of bootstrapping lies in its minimal assumptions and its applicability to a wide variety of statistical problems.

In applied data science, understanding sampling distributions and the behavior of estimators is crucial for interpreting the results of any analysis. Whether building predictive models, conducting A/B tests, or estimating population metrics, the reliability of conclusions depends on the quality of the underlying estimators and the accuracy with which their sampling distributions are understood. Mistaking the variability of an estimate for certainty can lead to overconfident decisions, while underestimating the power of well-designed sampling can result in missed opportunities for insight.

Sampling distributions and estimators thus lie at the intersection of theory and practice, enabling data scientists to connect raw observations to general truths. They provide the tools for measuring uncertainty, guiding inference, and validating models. Mastery of these concepts equips analysts with the ability to make sound, data-driven conclusions that stand up to scrutiny and that genuinely reflect the complexities of the populations they aim to understand.

Point Estimation and Properties

Point estimation is a foundational concept in statistics and data science, representing the practice of using sample data to estimate unknown parameters of a population. A point estimator is a single value, derived from the sample, that serves as the best guess for a population parameter such as the mean, variance, proportion, or standard deviation. This estimate is called a point estimate because it provides a specific numerical value rather than a range of plausible values. In many practical situations, point estimation is the first step in drawing statistical inferences, as it allows data scientists and analysts to summarize complex datasets into meaningful, interpretable quantities.

At the core of point estimation lies the challenge of making inferences from incomplete information. Since population parameters are often unknown and measuring every member of a population is usually impossible, we rely on samples to gain insight. From those samples, we use mathematical functions, known as estimators, to produce our best approximations of the true values we seek. For example, the sample mean is a point estimator for the population mean, and the sample proportion is used to estimate the population proportion. These estimators transform raw data into useful summaries that guide decision-making across fields such as economics, medicine, engineering, and public policy.

To evaluate the quality of a point estimator, statisticians use a set of desirable properties. One of the most important of these is unbiasedness. An estimator is considered unbiased if, on average, it produces the correct value of the parameter being estimated. This means that if we were to repeatedly draw samples and compute the estimate for each, the average of those estimates would equal the true parameter value. Unbiasedness ensures that there is no systematic overestimation or underestimation in the estimation process. For instance, the sample mean is an unbiased estimator of the population mean, and under certain conditions, the sample proportion is an unbiased estimator of the population proportion.

Another critical property is consistency. A consistent estimator converges to the true parameter value as the sample size increases. This means that with more data, the estimate becomes more accurate and reliable. Consistency reflects the idea that while small samples may yield noisy or unstable estimates, larger samples tend to produce estimates that are closer to the truth. This property is particularly important in real-world applications where increasing the sample size is often possible and desirable. Consistency provides the theoretical backing for the intuition that more data leads to better estimates, reinforcing the importance of collecting robust and representative samples in data science projects.

Efficiency is a third desirable characteristic of an estimator. Efficiency refers to the precision of an estimator, which is commonly measured by the variance of the estimator. Among all unbiased estimators of a given parameter, the one with the smallest variance is said to be the most efficient. An efficient estimator yields estimates that are consistently closer to the true parameter value than those produced by less efficient estimators. In practical terms, using an efficient estimator results in tighter confidence intervals and more powerful hypothesis tests. The quest for efficient estimators often leads statisticians to explore advanced methods such as maximum likelihood estimation or the method of moments.

Sufficiency is another important concept in point estimation. An estimator is sufficient if it captures all the information in the sample that is relevant to estimating the parameter. This means that no other statistic computed from the same sample can provide any additional insight about the parameter. Sufficiency is desirable because it ensures that the estimator is making full use of the data. In many cases, sufficient estimators are preferred not only for their completeness but also because they often lead to simpler and more elegant inference procedures. The concept of sufficiency is formalized using the factorization theorem and plays a significant role in theoretical statistics.

The method of constructing estimators is also crucial in determining their performance. One of the most widely used methods is the method of moments, which involves equating sample moments to population moments and solving the resulting equations for the parameter of interest. Another popular method is maximum likelihood estimation, which identifies the value of the parameter that maximizes the likelihood function—the probability of observing the given sample data under various parameter values. Maximum likelihood estimators often have appealing asymptotic properties, such as consistency and efficiency, and they form the basis for many advanced statistical techniques and machine learning models.

In practice, no single estimator is perfect in all situations. The choice of estimator often depends on the nature of the data, the sample size, the assumptions one is willing to make, and the goals of the analysis. For instance, in small samples, a biased estimator with low variance might be preferred over an unbiased estimator with high variance, especially when the bias is negligible and the reduction in variance improves the stability of results. This trade-off between bias and variance is central to many statistical and machine learning problems and is often visualized through the bias-variance trade-off curve.

Point estimation is not limited to simple one-parameter problems. In many real-world situations, multiple parameters must be estimated simultaneously, such as in linear regression, where the coefficients for several predictors are estimated together. Each of these coefficients represents a point estimate, and their joint behavior—especially their variance and covariance—plays a critical role in determining the overall reliability of the model. The estimators used in such models must be carefully chosen and interpreted in light of their underlying assumptions, such as linearity, independence, and homoscedasticity.

Moreover, point estimates should not be interpreted in isolation. Although they provide a concise summary, they carry no information about the uncertainty surrounding them. This is why point estimates are often accompanied by confidence intervals, which offer a range of plausible values for the parameter and reflect the variability inherent in the estimation process. Still, the point estimate remains the most direct and immediate summary of the data's implications for a parameter of interest, and its properties play a key role in shaping the confidence we have in our conclusions.

In the broader context of data science, point estimation forms the foundation of predictive modeling, data summarization, and decision-making under uncertainty. Whether estimating the average click-through rate of an online ad, the failure rate of a mechanical component, or the effect of a new drug, point estimators provide the quantitative basis for insight and action. Their properties determine the trustworthiness of these insights, making a deep understanding of point estimation not just a theoretical exercise, but a practical necessity in any serious engagement with data.

Confidence Intervals and Interpretation

Confidence intervals are a central concept in statistical inference, providing a method to express uncertainty about an estimated parameter. Unlike a point estimate, which gives a single best guess of a population parameter, a confidence interval offers a range of values that are believed to contain the true parameter with a specified level of confidence. This concept allows data scientists and statisticians to move beyond single-number summaries and to communicate the precision and reliability of their estimates in a probabilistic and informative way. Confidence intervals are indispensable in both exploratory and confirmatory analysis, serving as tools for estimation, comparison, and decision-making across a wide range of disciplines.

At its core, a confidence interval is constructed from sample data and is designed to capture the unknown population parameter in a proportion of repeated samples. For instance, a 95 percent confidence interval for the population mean implies that if we were to take many random samples and compute a 95 percent interval from each of them, approximately 95 percent of those intervals would contain the true population mean. It is important to understand that the confidence level does not refer to the probability that any one particular interval contains the parameter. Instead, it refers to the long-run performance of the interval construction method. The interval either contains the parameter or it does not, but over many repetitions, the procedure will be successful at the stated confidence rate.

The construction of a confidence interval typically involves three components: a point estimate, a measure of variability, and a critical value from a probability distribution. The point estimate represents the central value of the interval and is often the sample mean or proportion. The measure of variability is usually the standard error of the estimator, which quantifies how much the estimate is expected to vary from sample to sample. The critical value is derived from the sampling distribution and corresponds to the desired confidence level. For large samples or when the population distribution is normal, the standard normal distribution is often used. For smaller samples or when the population standard deviation is unknown, the t-distribution is more appropriate due to its heavier tails, which account for increased uncertainty.

The width of a confidence interval reflects the degree of uncertainty associated with the estimate. Narrow intervals indicate that the estimate is precise and that there is relatively little uncertainty about the parameter's value. Wide intervals suggest greater uncertainty and less precision. Several factors influence the width of a confidence interval, including the sample size, the variability in the data, and the chosen confidence level. Larger sample sizes reduce the standard error, resulting in narrower intervals. Higher variability in the data increases the standard error and therefore widens the interval. Choosing a higher confidence level, such as 99 percent instead of 95 percent, also produces a wider interval, as greater certainty requires accounting for a broader range of possible values.

Interpreting confidence intervals correctly is essential for sound statistical reasoning. One common misconception is that a 95 percent confidence interval means there is a 95 percent probability that the true parameter lies within the interval. This interpretation is incorrect because the parameter is fixed, not random. The randomness lies in the interval itself, which varies from sample to sample. A correct interpretation would be that the method used to calculate the interval has a 95 percent success rate in capturing the true parameter across many repetitions of the sampling process. Despite this subtlety, confidence intervals are immensely useful in practice, as they provide a straightforward way to assess the reliability of an estimate and to compare results across studies or groups.

Confidence intervals are widely used in scientific research, clinical trials, business analytics, and policy evaluation. In medical studies, for example, a confidence interval around the estimated effect of a new drug helps determine whether the effect is statistically significant and clinically meaningful. In survey research, confidence intervals around population proportions help assess public opinion with a known margin of error. In business, confidence intervals can guide strategic decisions by quantifying uncertainty in customer behavior, sales forecasts, or operational efficiency. Their versatility and interpretability make them a preferred method for expressing statistical uncertainty in virtually any domain involving data.

Confidence intervals also play a crucial role in hypothesis testing. If a confidence interval for a parameter excludes a value of interest—often the null hypothesis value—then the result is considered statistically significant at the corresponding confidence level. For instance, if a 95 percent confidence interval for a mean difference excludes zero, this indicates strong evidence against the null hypothesis of no difference. This duality between confidence intervals and hypothesis tests allows researchers to assess both the significance and the size of an effect in a single framework. Moreover, confidence intervals provide richer information than p-values alone, as they reveal not only whether an effect exists but also the range of values that the effect might plausibly take.

In regression analysis, confidence intervals are calculated for regression coefficients to evaluate the precision of the estimated relationships between predictors and the response variable. These intervals help identify which predictors have statistically significant effects and how much influence they may have. In time series forecasting, confidence intervals are used to produce prediction intervals, which indicate the range within which future observations are expected to fall with a given probability. In classification problems, intervals can be adapted into probability-based confidence estimates, helping to assess the certainty of classification decisions and the reliability of the model.

The construction and interpretation of confidence intervals depend on underlying assumptions, including random sampling, independence, and the correctness of the model or distributional assumptions. Violations of these assumptions can lead to misleading intervals that either overstate or understate the true level of uncertainty. Therefore, it is essential to validate these assumptions through diagnostic checks and to consider alternative methods, such as bootstrapping, when assumptions are questionable. Bootstrapping allows for the empirical construction of confidence intervals by resampling the data and computing the statistic of interest across many simulated samples. This technique is particularly valuable in complex or non-standard settings where analytical solutions are difficult to derive.

Confidence intervals are more than just statistical artifacts; they represent a fundamental way of communicating the limits of knowledge in data analysis. They emphasize that all data-driven conclusions carry uncertainty and that precision is as important as point estimates when interpreting results. By focusing attention on the range of plausible values, rather than single-number answers, confidence intervals encourage more thoughtful, cautious, and transparent reasoning in the face of incomplete information. They remind us that data science is not only about measurement and prediction, but also about understanding and expressing the uncertainty that inevitably accompanies those measurements and predictions.

Constructing Confidence Intervals

Constructing confidence intervals is one of the most practical and powerful techniques in inferential statistics. It enables analysts and researchers to estimate unknown population parameters by providing a range of plausible values, rather than relying on a single point estimate. This range reflects the level of uncertainty inherent in working with samples instead of entire populations. While point estimates can give an immediate summary of the data, confidence intervals account for sampling variability and allow for more informed and cautious interpretations. Understanding how confidence intervals are constructed is essential for any data scientist, as it forms the foundation of statistical inference in both academic research and applied analytics.

The process of constructing a confidence interval begins with identifying the parameter of interest and selecting an appropriate estimator. Common parameters include the population mean, proportion, difference in means, or regression coefficients. The estimator, such as the sample mean or sample proportion, provides the center of the confidence interval. Around this center, a margin of error is added and subtracted to form the interval bounds. The margin of error is determined by the standard error of the estimator and the critical value from a relevant probability distribution, typically the standard normal or t-distribution. The selection of the distribution depends on the sample size and whether the population standard deviation is known.

When constructing a confidence interval for the population mean with a known standard deviation, the standard normal distribution is used. In this case, the formula for a confidence interval is the sample mean plus or minus the critical value from the standard normal distribution multiplied by the standard error. The standard error is calculated by dividing the population standard deviation by the square root of the sample size. The critical value corresponds to the desired confidence level, such as 1.96 for a 95 percent confidence interval. This value represents the number of standard errors required to capture the central proportion of the sampling distribution.

However, in most real-world situations, the population standard deviation is unknown, and the t-distribution is used instead. The t-distribution is similar in shape to the normal distribution but has heavier tails, which provide more conservative estimates to account for the additional uncertainty from estimating the standard deviation. The formula remains structurally similar, but the critical value is taken from the t-distribution with degrees of freedom equal to the sample size minus one. As the sample size increases, the t-distribution approaches the normal distribution, and the difference between the two becomes negligible. This adjustment makes the t-distribution especially important for small-sample inference.

For proportions, confidence intervals are constructed using the sample proportion as the estimator and the standard error derived from the binomial distribution. The standard error for a proportion is the square root of the product of the proportion and its complement divided by the sample size. This approach assumes a sufficiently large sample so that the binomial distribution can be approximated by the normal distribution. If the sample size is small or the proportion is near zero or one, alternative methods such as the Wilson score interval or the exact Clopper-Pearson interval may be more appropriate, as they provide better coverage properties under these conditions.

When estimating the difference between two means, such as in comparing two treatment groups, the construction of a confidence interval becomes slightly more complex. The estimator is the difference between the two sample means, and the standard error depends on the variances and sizes of both samples. If the variances are assumed to be equal, a pooled estimate of the variance is used. Otherwise, a separate-variances approach is applied, often with degrees of freedom calculated using the Welch-Satterthwaite equation. The critical value is again drawn from the t-distribution, and the resulting interval provides insight into whether the observed difference is statistically meaningful or likely to have occurred by random chance.

Confidence intervals can also be constructed for regression coefficients in linear models. After fitting a regression model, each coefficient is associated with an estimated standard error, which measures the variability in that estimate across repeated samples. A confidence interval for a coefficient is calculated in the same way as for a mean: the estimated coefficient plus or minus the critical value from the t-distribution times its standard error. These intervals help determine which predictors have statistically significant effects on the outcome and provide a sense of the precision of those effects.

An important part of constructing confidence intervals is choosing the confidence level, which reflects how certain we want to be that the interval contains the true parameter. Common confidence levels are 90 percent, 95 percent, and 99 percent. Higher confidence levels produce wider intervals, as they require capturing a larger portion of the sampling distribution. The choice of confidence level should be guided by the context and consequences of decision-making. In high-stakes applications, such as medical trials or safety assessments, higher confidence may be preferred, while in exploratory research, narrower intervals with slightly lower confidence may be acceptable.

The quality of a confidence interval also depends on the validity of the assumptions underlying the estimation process. Assumptions such as independence of observations, normality of the sampling distribution, and accurate estimation of variability are critical for ensuring the reliability of the interval. Violations of these assumptions can lead to incorrect intervals that do not maintain their nominal coverage rate. Diagnostic tools such as normal probability plots, residual analysis, and variance checks are often used to assess whether the conditions for valid inference are met.

When assumptions are questionable or standard methods are inappropriate, resampling techniques like bootstrapping can be employed to construct confidence intervals. Bootstrapping involves repeatedly drawing samples with replacement from the observed data and recalculating the estimator each time. The distribution of these bootstrap estimates approximates the sampling distribution, and percentiles from this distribution can be used to construct a confidence interval. This nonparametric approach is especially useful for complex estimators, small samples, or data with unknown distributions, as it requires fewer assumptions about the underlying population.

Constructing confidence intervals is not just a mechanical process of plugging values into formulas. It requires judgment about which method to use, how to interpret the result, and what implications the interval has for the broader question at hand. Confidence intervals help quantify the uncertainty in estimates, guide comparisons between groups, and support evidence-based decision-making. They provide more nuanced insight than binary hypothesis tests and encourage thinking in terms of ranges and probabilities rather than fixed conclusions. By mastering the construction and interpretation of confidence intervals, data scientists and statisticians can communicate their findings more effectively and make more informed, reliable inferences from data.

Bayesian vs Frequentist Perspectives

The contrast between Bayesian and Frequentist perspectives lies at the heart of statistical thinking, shaping how data is interpreted, how uncertainty is modeled, and how conclusions are drawn. Both frameworks aim to infer truths about the world from observed data, but they do so based on fundamentally different philosophies. This divergence influences everything from the interpretation of probability to the methods used for estimation and hypothesis testing. While they often produce similar results in large samples or under certain assumptions, the ways in which they reach those results and the meaning attached to them can be strikingly different.

At the core of the Frequentist view is the idea that probability is defined through the long-run frequency of events. In this approach, parameters are considered fixed but unknown quantities, and randomness arises solely through the sampling process. A Frequentist does not assign probabilities to parameters themselves because they are not treated as random variables. Instead, probability statements are made about the likelihood of observing certain data given fixed parameters. This perspective leads to concepts such as confidence intervals and p-values, which describe the behavior of estimators and test statistics under repeated sampling from the same population.

In contrast, the Bayesian perspective treats probability as a degree of belief or certainty about an event or hypothesis. From this viewpoint, parameters are considered random variables, and probability represents subjective uncertainty about their true values. Bayesian analysis begins with a prior distribution, which encodes the analyst's beliefs about a parameter before observing the data. This prior is then updated using the likelihood of the observed data to produce a posterior distribution, which reflects updated beliefs after taking the data into account. The result is a full probability distribution over the parameter, from which credible intervals and probability statements can be directly derived.

One of the most profound differences between these paradigms lies in their treatment of uncertainty. In the Frequentist framework, uncertainty comes from the randomness inherent in the sampling process. If an experiment were repeated many times, different samples would yield different estimates, and Frequentist methods characterize this variability. A confidence interval, for instance, is defined by the proportion of such intervals that would contain the true parameter value over many repetitions. It does not allow us to say there is a specific probability that the true parameter lies within any one interval. By contrast, the Bayesian credible interval offers a direct probabilistic interpretation: given the observed data and the chosen prior, there is a specified probability that the parameter lies within the interval. This difference in interpretation has significant implications for how results are communicated and understood.

The use of prior information is another key distinction. Frequentist methods aim to be objective and rely exclusively on the data collected in the current study. This makes them appealing in contexts where analysts want results to reflect only the observed data, free from external influences. However, this also means they can be inefficient or unstable when data is sparse or noisy. Bayesian methods, by incorporating prior knowledge, can stabilize estimates and yield more reasonable results in small-sample settings or in highly uncertain environments. The prior can be informed by previous research, expert opinion, or theoretical considerations. While this can enhance inference, it also introduces subjectivity and potential bias, especially if the prior is poorly chosen or overly influential.

Bayesian methods also provide a more coherent approach to decision-making under uncertainty. Because they generate a full probability distribution over parameters or hypotheses, Bayesian analyses can directly compute the expected utility or risk associated with different choices. This makes them particularly useful in areas such as medical decision-making, economics, and machine learning, where trade-offs between competing options must be carefully balanced. Frequentist methods, while offering powerful tools for estimation and hypothesis testing, often require more complex or indirect procedures to make similar decisions.

In hypothesis testing, the differences between the two schools of thought are especially apparent. Frequentist tests rely on p-values, which measure the probability of observing data as extreme or more extreme than what was observed, assuming the null hypothesis is true. A small p-value suggests the data is unlikely under the null and leads to its rejection. However, this logic is sometimes counterintuitive and widely misunderstood. A common misinterpretation is that the p-value represents the probability that the null hypothesis is true, which it does not. In contrast, Bayesian hypothesis testing compares the posterior probabilities of competing hypotheses directly, often through a quantity known as the Bayes factor. This allows for a more intuitive interpretation: how strongly does the data support one hypothesis over

47

another, given the prior beliefs?

The computational demands of Bayesian analysis have historically been a barrier to its widespread use. Calculating posterior distributions often requires complex integrations that are difficult or impossible to solve analytically. However, advances in computing power and the development of numerical techniques such as Markov Chain Monte Carlo methods have made Bayesian approaches much more accessible. These tools allow analysts to approximate posterior distributions for complex models and to apply Bayesian inference in high-dimensional and real-time settings, making it a practical and flexible framework for modern data science.

Despite their differences, Bayesian and Frequentist methods are not mutually exclusive. In fact, many practitioners use elements of both approaches depending on the problem at hand. Bayesian methods excel in situations where prior knowledge is strong, data is limited, or full probability distributions are needed for decision-making. Frequentist methods are well-suited for standardized testing, large-scale data analysis, and scenarios where objectivity and reproducibility are paramount. Both perspectives contribute to the rich landscape of statistical methodology and offer valuable insights into the nature of evidence, uncertainty, and inference.

The choice between Bayesian and Frequentist approaches often reflects philosophical orientation, the context of the problem, and practical considerations such as computational resources or the availability of prior information. For data scientists, a deep understanding of both perspectives enables more nuanced and effective analysis. It encourages critical thinking about the assumptions underlying different methods and promotes flexibility in applying the most appropriate tools for each unique situation. Ultimately, the strength of statistical reasoning lies not in strict adherence to one school of thought but in the ability to navigate between them with clarity, rigor, and purpose.

Prior Distributions and Beliefs

In Bayesian statistics, prior distributions play a critical role in shaping the outcome of an analysis. They represent the beliefs, knowledge, or assumptions held about an unknown parameter before any data is observed. Unlike the frequentist approach, which treats parameters as fixed and unknown, the Bayesian perspective views them as random variables with their own probability distributions. The prior distribution is the mathematical expression of what is known or assumed about the parameter before the influence of new evidence. This idea introduces a flexible and powerful framework for incorporating previous knowledge into statistical inference, enabling analysts to formalize experience, theoretical understanding, or domain expertise into the modeling process.

The use of prior distributions allows the Bayesian framework to continuously update beliefs as new data becomes available. This updating process is governed by Bayes' theorem, which combines the prior distribution with the likelihood of the observed data to produce a posterior distribution. The posterior distribution reflects the updated beliefs after taking the data into account. This dynamic mechanism for learning from data distinguishes Bayesian inference from other forms of statistical reasoning. The ability to start with an initial belief, observe evidence, and revise that belief in a coherent, quantitative manner mirrors the way humans intuitively learn from experience.

Choosing an appropriate prior distribution is both an art and a science. The choice depends on the context of the problem, the availability of prior information, and the goals of the analysis. Priors can be informative, weakly informative, or non-informative. An informative prior incorporates substantial prior knowledge or strong assumptions about the parameter. For example, in clinical research, prior studies might provide clear estimates of a treatment effect, which can be used to construct a tightly concentrated prior distribution. A weakly informative prior expresses general expectations without being overly restrictive, such as assuming that a parameter is positive but allowing for a broad range of values. Non-informative or flat priors are used when little or no prior information is available. These priors are designed to have minimal influence on the posterior distribution, allowing the data to speak more freely.

The selection of a prior should be justified carefully, especially in scientific and policy contexts where conclusions can have significant implications. An inappropriate or overly influential prior can bias the results, leading to misleading inferences. At the same time, a well-chosen prior can stabilize estimation in small-sample scenarios or when data is sparse or noisy. This is particularly valuable in real-world settings where perfect data is rarely available. Priors can prevent overfitting, improve model convergence, and incorporate important constraints that reflect real-world limitations or scientific theories.

Priors are often chosen from families of distributions that are mathematically convenient or that have conjugate relationships with the likelihood. A conjugate prior is one that, when combined with a particular likelihood function, yields a posterior distribution in the same family as the prior. This property simplifies computation and facilitates analytical solutions. For example, the beta distribution is a conjugate prior for the binomial likelihood, and the normal distribution is conjugate to itself under a normal likelihood. Conjugate priors are commonly used in analytical work and teaching because they lead to closed-form posterior distributions. However, modern computational techniques such as Markov Chain Monte Carlo have made it possible to use more flexible and realistic priors, even when they lack conjugate properties.

Subjectivity is a common criticism of the Bayesian use of priors, especially in scientific disciplines that value objectivity and replicability. Critics argue that priors introduce personal beliefs into the analysis, making results less transparent or harder to generalize. However, Bayesian proponents counter that all statistical models involve assumptions, whether explicit or implicit. Priors at least force those assumptions to be stated clearly and allow for their impact to be examined and debated. Moreover, sensitivity analysis can be conducted to explore how different priors affect the posterior results. This practice helps ensure that conclusions are robust and that inferences do not depend unduly on arbitrary prior choices.

The flexibility of priors allows them to be tailored to specific problems. In hierarchical models, priors can be assigned at multiple levels of the model, reflecting uncertainty not only about parameters but also about hyperparameters. These hierarchical priors are especially useful in complex systems or multi-level data structures, where parameters vary across groups or contexts. In model selection and machine learning, priors are used to regularize parameter estimates and prevent overfitting. Techniques such as Bayesian ridge regression and the use of sparsity-inducing priors like the Laplace distribution demonstrate how prior beliefs can guide the learning process and improve generalization to new data.

Empirical Bayes methods offer a hybrid approach in which the prior is estimated from the data itself. This can be useful when prior information is not available in advance but can be inferred from a large or structured dataset. While this approach blurs the line between prior and likelihood, it often yields practical benefits and has found applications in genomics, natural language processing, and recommendation systems. It is important, however, to recognize that using the data to construct the prior may affect the theoretical properties of the analysis and should be done with care.

In addition to shaping the inference itself, priors play an important role in Bayesian decision theory. By combining the posterior distribution with a utility or loss function, decision makers can calculate the expected utility of different actions and choose the one that maximizes expected benefit. This makes Bayesian methods particularly attractive in fields such as medicine, finance, and engineering, where decisions must be made under uncertainty and where trade-offs between outcomes are explicit and quantifiable.

The philosophical foundation of Bayesian analysis rests on the idea that knowledge is uncertain and that rational inference involves updating beliefs in light of evidence. Prior distributions formalize this uncertainty and provide a mechanism for learning from data in a coherent and transparent manner. Far from being a limitation, the use of priors reflects the reality that data does not exist in a vacuum. All data analysis is conducted in a context, informed by theory, experience, or expert judgment. Prior distributions make that context visible, allowing it to be incorporated, evaluated, and revised as part of the analytical process. By embracing this approach, Bayesian methods offer a richer and more flexible framework for understanding the world through data.

Bayesian Updating with Data

Bayesian updating is the core mechanism by which Bayesian inference incorporates new data into existing beliefs. It is the mathematical embodiment of learning from experience, allowing analysts to refine their understanding of uncertain quantities as additional evidence becomes available. This process is governed by Bayes' theorem, a deceptively simple formula with profound implications for reasoning under uncertainty. At its heart, Bayesian updating transforms a prior distribution, which reflects beliefs about a parameter before seeing the data, into a posterior distribution, which incorporates the new evidence and represents the updated belief. This process is continuous and dynamic, making Bayesian methods especially well-suited for real-time learning, adaptive modeling, and decision-making in uncertain environments.

The mathematical foundation of Bayesian updating lies in Bayes' theorem, which states that the posterior probability of a hypothesis given observed data is proportional to the likelihood of the data under that hypothesis multiplied by the prior probability of the hypothesis. In symbolic form, the posterior is equal to the product of the prior and the likelihood, divided by a normalization constant that ensures the posterior distribution sums or integrates to one. This normalization factor, called the marginal likelihood or evidence, is obtained by summing or integrating the numerator across all possible values of the parameter. Though often complex in practice, this operation ensures that the resulting posterior distribution is a valid probability distribution that reflects the revised beliefs after accounting for the data.

To understand how Bayesian updating works, consider a simple example involving a binomial process. Suppose we are estimating the probability of success in a series of coin tosses. Before observing any data, we might assign a prior distribution to this unknown probability, reflecting our initial belief. A common choice is the beta distribution, which serves as a conjugate prior for the binomial likelihood. Once we observe the outcomes of the coin tosses, we compute the likelihood of the observed data under different values of the success probability.

Multiplying the prior and the likelihood yields an unnormalized posterior, which is then normalized to form the updated distribution. This posterior reflects our new belief about the success probability, incorporating both the prior information and the observed evidence.

One of the key features of Bayesian updating is its cumulative nature. Each new piece of data refines the posterior, and the posterior from one round of updating becomes the prior for the next. This allows for sequential analysis, where data arrives over time and the model continually evolves. In applications such as online learning, streaming data analysis, or sensor fusion, this sequential updating process enables real-time decision-making and adaptive modeling. Rather than discarding old data or starting over with each update, the Bayesian framework efficiently incorporates new information while retaining the influence of past observations.

The influence of the prior diminishes as more data is observed. In the early stages of analysis, when data is scarce, the prior has a strong effect on the posterior distribution. This is desirable when prior knowledge is reliable and can help guide inference in the face of limited information. However, as the sample size increases, the likelihood becomes more dominant, and the posterior converges toward the true parameter value regardless of the prior, provided the prior is not completely inconsistent with the data. This property ensures that Bayesian methods are not unduly influenced by subjective beliefs in the long run, while still allowing those beliefs to play a constructive role in small-sample contexts.

Bayesian updating is also highly adaptable to complex and hierarchical models. In multilevel structures, where parameters vary across groups or levels, updating can occur at each level of the model. This allows for partial pooling of information across different units, improving estimation accuracy and borrowing strength from related observations. For example, in medical research comparing the effectiveness of treatments across hospitals, a hierarchical Bayesian model can update treatment effects both within each hospital and across the entire system, accounting for shared variance and individual differences simultaneously.

In addition to parameter estimation, Bayesian updating is used extensively in model selection and averaging. Rather than choosing a single best model, the Bayesian approach assigns probabilities to multiple models and updates these probabilities as data is observed. This process, known as Bayesian model averaging, accounts for model uncertainty and improves predictive performance by weighting forecasts according to their posterior model probabilities. In fields like econometrics, epidemiology, and machine learning, where multiple plausible models often compete, this approach provides a principled way to incorporate uncertainty into model-based predictions.

Computational techniques are often required to carry out Bayesian updating, especially when dealing with high-dimensional or non-conjugate models. Markov Chain Monte Carlo methods, such as the Metropolis-Hastings algorithm or Gibbs sampling, allow for approximate posterior sampling when analytic solutions are infeasible. These algorithms generate samples from the posterior distribution by constructing a Markov chain that explores the parameter space according to a stationary distribution matching the posterior. By collecting a large number of samples, analysts can approximate the shape of the posterior, compute credible intervals, and make probabilistic predictions. More recent developments in variational inference and Hamiltonian Monte Carlo have further expanded the scalability and efficiency of Bayesian updating in modern applications.

Bayesian updating is also deeply intuitive. It reflects a natural cognitive process of adjusting beliefs in response to new evidence. When humans revise their expectations after seeing new outcomes, they are unconsciously performing a form of Bayesian inference. This correspondence between statistical theory and human reasoning contributes to the appeal of the Bayesian framework, especially in disciplines where interpretability and transparency are important. It provides a coherent methodology for tracking how evidence changes beliefs, enabling analysts to articulate not only what they believe but also why they believe it and how their beliefs evolve over time.

In real-world applications, Bayesian updating supports dynamic systems that must respond to changing conditions. In finance, trading algorithms update risk assessments based on market movements. In robotics, autonomous systems refine their maps and plans as new sensor data becomes available. In healthcare, Bayesian updating allows practitioners to revise diagnostic probabilities as test results are gathered. The ability to continuously refine inferences in the presence of uncertainty and new data makes Bayesian updating an indispensable tool in domains that require flexible, adaptive intelligence.

Ultimately, Bayesian updating embodies the principle of learning through evidence. It transforms the static act of estimation into a living process of belief revision, anchored in probability and guided by data. This dynamic perspective not only deepens the understanding of uncertainty but also enhances the ability to act under uncertainty. By merging prior knowledge with observed reality in a mathematically rigorous way, Bayesian updating enables smarter, more responsive, and more transparent decision-making in the ever-evolving world of data.

Maximum Likelihood Estimation

Maximum Likelihood Estimation, often abbreviated as MLE, is one of the most widely used methods in statistical inference for estimating the parameters of a probabilistic model. The core idea behind MLE is to find the parameter values that make the observed data most probable under a given statistical model. This approach is grounded in the likelihood function, which measures how likely it is to observe the given data for various possible values of the model parameters. By maximizing this function, we obtain the parameter estimates that best explain the data according to the assumptions of the model. MLE is appealing not only for its intuitive logic but also for its strong theoretical properties and its flexibility in a broad range of applications, from classical statistics to modern machine learning.

The likelihood function plays a central role in MLE. Given a set of independent and identically distributed observations and a statistical model that specifies a probability distribution for those observations, the likelihood is defined as the joint probability of the observed data as a function of the unknown parameters. It is important to note that while the probability function is typically viewed as a function of the data for a fixed parameter, the likelihood function reverses this relationship, treating the data as fixed and the parameters as variable. This shift in perspective allows us to use the observed data to evaluate how plausible different parameter values are and to identify the most likely ones.

To perform maximum likelihood estimation, the first step is to specify the form of the likelihood function based on the assumed distribution of the data. For example, if the data are assumed to follow a normal distribution, the likelihood function will be derived from the normal probability density function. Once the likelihood function is defined, the goal is to find the parameter values that maximize it. In practice, it is often more convenient to work with the log-likelihood, which is the natural logarithm of the likelihood function. Because the logarithm is a monotonic transformation, maximizing the log-likelihood yields the same parameter estimates as maximizing the likelihood itself. The log-likelihood has the advantage of simplifying the mathematics, especially when dealing with products of probabilities, which become sums of logarithms.

Maximizing the log-likelihood typically involves taking the derivative with respect to each parameter, setting the resulting equations equal to zero, and solving for the parameters. These solutions, known as the maximum likelihood estimates, provide the values that best fit the data under the model. In some cases, the equations can be solved analytically, leading to closed-form expressions for the estimates. In more complex models, numerical optimization methods such as gradient ascent, Newton-Raphson, or expectation-maximization may be required. These iterative algorithms start from an initial guess and update the estimates step by step until the likelihood function is maximized.

One of the strengths of maximum likelihood estimation is its desirable statistical properties under general conditions. MLEs are consistent, meaning they converge to the true parameter values as the sample size increases. They are also asymptotically normal, which means that for large samples, the distribution of the estimator approaches a normal distribution centered at the true parameter value with a variance that can be estimated from the data. Additionally, MLEs are asymptotically efficient, achieving the lowest possible variance among all unbiased estimators in large samples. These properties make MLE a powerful tool for inference, especially in settings where large amounts of data are available.

MLE is also highly flexible and can be applied to a wide range of models and data types. Whether dealing with continuous variables, discrete outcomes, censored data, or hierarchical structures, the likelihood framework can accommodate various complexities by appropriately specifying the form of the likelihood function. In generalized linear models, for example, MLE is used to estimate the regression coefficients for models that include logistic, Poisson, or exponential distributions. In time series analysis, MLE is employed to fit autoregressive and moving average models. In survival analysis, MLE handles censored data by modifying the likelihood function to account for partial information. This adaptability is one of the key reasons why MLE remains a cornerstone of modern statistical practice.

Despite its strengths, MLE is not without limitations. One of the main concerns is the reliance on the correct specification of the model. If the assumed probability distribution does not match the true data-generating process, the MLE can be biased or misleading. This issue, known as model misspecification, highlights the importance of model diagnostics and validation in any statistical analysis. Another potential drawback is the sensitivity of MLE to outliers. Because the method seeks to maximize the likelihood of the entire dataset, extreme values can disproportionately influence the estimates, especially in small samples. Robust alternatives, such as M-estimators or Bayesian methods with prior regularization, may be preferable when data quality is questionable or when robustness is a concern.

The likelihood framework also provides a basis for model comparison and hypothesis testing. The likelihood ratio test, for instance, compares the fit of two nested models by evaluating the ratio of their maximum likelihoods. Under regularity conditions, the test statistic follows a chi-square distribution, allowing for the assessment of whether the more complex model significantly improves the fit. Information criteria such as AIC and BIC also derive from the likelihood, penalizing model complexity to avoid overfitting while rewarding goodness of fit. These tools extend the utility of MLE beyond point estimation to broader tasks in model selection and evaluation.

In machine learning, MLE often serves as the foundation for training probabilistic models. Many supervised learning algorithms, such as logistic regression and naive Bayes classifiers, are formulated to maximize the likelihood of the observed labels given the input features. In unsupervised learning, models like Gaussian mixture models or hidden Markov models rely on MLE to estimate the underlying structure of the data. The expectation-maximization algorithm, in particular, provides an efficient way to perform MLE in models with latent variables. The influence of MLE extends even to deep learning, where loss functions such as cross-entropy are directly related to the negative log-likelihood.

Maximum Likelihood Estimation exemplifies the synergy between theory and application in statistics. It combines a clear, intuitive rationale with rigorous mathematical foundations and practical flexibility. Whether estimating simple parameters, fitting complex models, or comparing competing hypotheses, MLE offers a systematic approach to extracting meaning from data. Its robustness in large samples and adaptability to various settings ensure its continued relevance in the evolving landscape of data science, where precise and interpretable inference remains essential.

Likelihood Functions and Optimization

The likelihood function is a cornerstone of statistical inference and plays a central role in parameter estimation, model fitting, and decision-making. It is the mathematical tool that quantifies how well different parameter values explain the observed data under a given statistical model. Unlike a probability distribution, which describes the likelihood of data given fixed parameters, the likelihood function reverses the roles by treating the observed data as fixed and the parameters as variable. This distinction is subtle but critical, as it allows analysts to explore the plausibility of various parameter configurations and to identify those that best explain the data. Optimization, in turn, is the mathematical process used to find the values of the parameters that maximize the likelihood function, making it an essential part of likelihood-based inference.

Formally, the likelihood function is defined as the joint probability of the observed data expressed as a function of the parameters of the model. For a set of independent and identically distributed observations, the likelihood is typically written as the product of the individual probability density or mass functions evaluated at each data point. Because this product can involve a large number of terms, it is common to work with the logarithm of the likelihood, known as the log-likelihood. The log-likelihood transforms the product into a sum, which is numerically more stable and easier to manipulate. Maximizing the log-likelihood yields the same parameter estimates as maximizing the original likelihood function because the logarithm is a monotonic transformation.

Maximizing the likelihood function is a key task in statistical modeling and is most commonly associated with the method of Maximum Likelihood Estimation. The goal is to find the parameter values that make the observed data most probable under the model. In simple cases, such as estimating the mean of a normally distributed variable with known variance, the optimization can be performed analytically by taking derivatives, setting them equal to zero, and solving for the parameters. However, in many real-world applications, the likelihood function is complex, involving multiple parameters, nonlinear relationships, or latent variables. In such cases, optimization must be carried out numerically using iterative algorithms that approximate the maximum of the function.

Gradient-based optimization methods are commonly used for maximizing likelihood functions. These methods rely on the gradient, or the vector of partial derivatives of the log-likelihood with respect to each parameter. The gradient points in the direction of the steepest increase of the function, and iterative algorithms such as gradient ascent or Newton-Raphson use this information to update the parameter estimates. In each iteration, the algorithm moves the parameters slightly in the direction suggested by the gradient, gradually climbing the likelihood surface toward a local or global maximum. The Newton-Raphson method further incorporates second-order information from the Hessian matrix, which contains the second derivatives of the log-likelihood, allowing for faster and more accurate convergence in well-behaved functions.

In practice, the likelihood surface may be irregular, with multiple local maxima, flat regions, or steep cliffs. These features can complicate the optimization process, making it challenging to find the true maximum or to ensure that the algorithm converges at all. To address these issues, optimization routines often incorporate strategies such as step size adjustment, momentum, or stochastic sampling. For example, stochastic gradient ascent uses randomly selected subsets of the data, called mini-batches, to estimate the gradient at each iteration. This reduces computational burden and introduces noise that can help escape local maxima, making it especially useful in large-scale machine learning applications.

Likelihood functions are not only used for point estimation but also for constructing interval estimates and conducting hypothesis tests. The curvature of the log-likelihood function near its maximum provides information about the precision of the parameter estimates. Specifically, the inverse of the observed Fisher information, which is the negative second derivative of the log-likelihood, gives an estimate of the variance of the estimator. This quantity is used to construct confidence intervals around the maximum likelihood estimates, providing a measure of uncertainty. Additionally, likelihood ratio tests compare the maximum values of the likelihood function under different models, enabling formal tests of hypotheses such as whether a parameter equals zero or whether one model fits the data significantly better than another.

In more complex models involving latent variables or hierarchical structures, direct maximization of the likelihood function becomes more challenging. The Expectation-Maximization algorithm is a widely used approach for handling such cases. It alternates between an expectation step, which computes the expected log-likelihood given the current parameter estimates, and a maximization step, which updates the parameters to maximize this expected value. This iterative process converges to a local maximum of the likelihood function and is especially useful in applications such as mixture models, hidden Markov models, and missing data problems.

The shape of the likelihood function also provides diagnostic insights into the model and data. A sharply peaked likelihood surface indicates strong information about the parameters, while a flat surface suggests that the data are not very informative or that the model is poorly specified. Likelihood profiles, which plot the likelihood function as a function of one parameter while holding others fixed, can help identify parameter identifiability issues and assess the sensitivity of the estimates to changes in the model. These tools are valuable for model validation and refinement, guiding the analyst toward more accurate and interpretable conclusions.

Computational tools have made it possible to perform likelihood-based inference in a wide range of settings. Statistical software packages offer built-in functions for specifying models, computing likelihoods, and performing optimization. These tools often include safeguards to detect convergence problems, check gradient norms, and evaluate the quality of the solution. As models become more complex and data sets grow larger, efficient likelihood evaluation and optimization become increasingly critical. Advances in algorithm design, parallel computing, and automatic differentiation continue to expand the frontier of what is computationally feasible in likelihood-based inference.

Likelihood functions and optimization are not merely technical procedures but are essential to the practice of data science. They allow analysts to construct models that reflect underlying mechanisms, estimate parameters with rigor, and make predictions grounded in probabilistic reasoning. By maximizing the compatibility between the model and the observed data, likelihood-based methods provide a principled approach to extracting knowledge from uncertainty. Whether in scientific research, machine learning, or operational decision-making, the combination of likelihood functions and optimization forms the engine that drives much of modern statistical analysis.

Sufficiency and Efficiency of Estimators

Sufficiency and efficiency are two of the most important properties used to evaluate the quality of estimators in statistical inference. These concepts help determine how well an estimator captures the information contained in the data and how precisely it estimates the parameter of interest. Together, they provide a rigorous framework for comparing different estimators and guiding the selection of optimal methods for estimation. While they originate from classical statistics, these principles continue to inform modern data science, particularly in the design and evaluation of models, the development of algorithms, and the interpretation of uncertainty.

The concept of sufficiency is grounded in the idea of information preservation. A statistic is said to be sufficient for a parameter if it contains all the information in the sample that is relevant for estimating that parameter. In other words, once the value of a sufficient statistic is known, no additional information about the parameter can be gained by examining the rest of the sample. Sufficiency allows for data reduction without loss of information, making it a powerful concept in both theory and practice. For example, in a sample drawn from a normal distribution with known variance, the sample mean is a sufficient statistic for the population mean. This means that the sample mean captures all the information in the data that pertains to the mean, and any further analysis of the sample will not improve the estimate of that parameter.

Sufficiency is formally defined using the factorization theorem, which provides a criterion for determining whether a statistic is sufficient. According to this theorem, a statistic is sufficient for a parameter if the likelihood function can be factored into two parts: one that depends on the data only through the statistic, and another that does not depend on the parameter at all. This characterization not only aids in identifying sufficient statistics but also plays a key role in developing optimal estimation procedures. By reducing the data to a sufficient statistic, statisticians can simplify complex problems and focus inference on the most relevant quantities.

Beyond sufficiency, the quality of an estimator is also judged by its efficiency. Efficiency refers to the precision of an estimator, typically measured in terms of its variance. An efficient estimator has the smallest possible variance among all unbiased estimators of a parameter, making it the most reliable estimator in repeated sampling. Efficiency is especially important when data is limited or when precise estimates are critical for decision-making. The Cramér-Rao lower bound provides a theoretical benchmark for efficiency, establishing the minimum variance that any unbiased estimator can achieve for a given parameter and data distribution. An estimator that reaches this lower bound is said to be efficient.

In many classical estimation problems, the maximum likelihood estimator is not only consistent and asymptotically normal but also asymptotically efficient, meaning that it approaches the Cramér-Rao lower bound as the sample size grows. This property underscores the widespread use of maximum likelihood estimation in statistical modeling. However, efficiency can vary across different estimators and settings. An estimator that is efficient in one context may not be in another, especially if the underlying assumptions of the model are violated. This variability highlights the importance of context-specific evaluation and the potential trade-offs between different estimator properties.

Sufficiency and efficiency are often complementary, but they are not the same. A statistic can be sufficient without being efficient, and an efficient estimator may not be based on a sufficient statistic. However, under certain regularity conditions, the Rao-Blackwell theorem shows that any unbiased estimator can be improved by conditioning it on a sufficient statistic. The resulting estimator has a variance that is less than or equal to the original estimator, and if the sufficient statistic is complete, the improved estimator is unique and optimal. This result provides a powerful method for constructing efficient estimators from simpler, perhaps less efficient ones.

The concept of completeness, closely related to sufficiency, further refines the search for optimal estimators. A sufficient statistic is complete if no non-zero function of the statistic has an expected value of zero for all values of the parameter. Completeness ensures that the sufficient statistic is not only informative but also rich enough to capture all variation in the parameter. When a sufficient statistic is both sufficient and complete, it becomes the foundation for the unique minimum variance unbiased estimator, also known as the MVUE. This estimator is considered optimal under the criterion of unbiasedness and minimum variance.

In practice, identifying sufficient and efficient estimators helps improve the interpretability and reliability of statistical analysis. For example, in survey sampling, using sufficient statistics allows analysts to summarize data in a way that retains all relevant information about the target population. In regression analysis, the ordinary least squares estimator is efficient under the Gauss-Markov assumptions, making it the best linear unbiased estimator of the regression coefficients. In time series analysis, maximum likelihood estimation often leads to efficient parameter estimates when the model is correctly specified. These applications demonstrate how the theoretical properties of estimators translate into practical advantages in real-world analysis.

In computational statistics and machine learning, the principles of sufficiency and efficiency influence algorithm design and evaluation. For instance, when training models on large datasets, sufficient statistics can be used to reduce computational burden without sacrificing accuracy. In distributed computing environments, sufficient statistics enable efficient aggregation of information across different nodes. Similarly, in probabilistic programming and Bayesian inference, using sufficient statistics simplifies posterior computation and accelerates convergence. The idea of efficiency also informs model selection, where trade-offs between model complexity and estimation variance must be carefully balanced.

As data science continues to evolve, the foundational concepts of sufficiency and efficiency remain as relevant as ever. They provide a rigorous basis for understanding the behavior of estimators, guiding the development of new methodologies and ensuring the integrity of statistical conclusions. Whether applied in traditional statistical models or cutting-edge machine learning algorithms, these principles help ensure that inference is both informative and reliable. By striving for sufficiency, analysts make full use of the data, and by aiming for efficiency, they achieve the highest precision possible given the constraints of the problem. This dual focus leads to statistical procedures that are not only theoretically sound but also practically effective across a wide range of applications.

Hypothesis Testing Framework

Hypothesis testing is a fundamental framework in statistical inference used to assess the plausibility of assumptions or claims about a population based on sample data. It provides a structured method for making decisions under uncertainty, offering a systematic way to evaluate evidence and quantify the strength of that evidence. The core idea behind hypothesis testing is to formulate two competing hypotheses and then use statistical methods to determine which one is more consistent with the observed data. This approach is essential in fields ranging from medicine and economics to engineering and social sciences, where researchers and practitioners routinely face questions about differences, associations, and effects that must be tested using data.

At the center of the hypothesis testing framework are two hypotheses: the null hypothesis and the alternative hypothesis. The null hypothesis, typically denoted as H_o, represents the default assumption or status quo. It often posits that there is no effect, no difference, or no association in the population. For example, in a clinical trial comparing two treatments, the null hypothesis might state that both treatments have the same average effectiveness. The alternative hypothesis, denoted as H_1 or H_a, represents a competing claim, suggesting that there is an effect, a difference, or an association. Continuing with the clinical example, the alternative hypothesis would assert that one treatment is more effective than the other.

Once the hypotheses are established, the next step is to choose an appropriate test statistic. This statistic is a function of the sample data and is designed to summarize the evidence against the null hypothesis. The choice of test statistic depends on the nature of the data and the hypotheses being tested. Common test statistics include the z-score, t-score, chi-square statistic, and F-ratio. Each of these has an associated sampling distribution under the assumption that the null hypothesis is true. By comparing the observed value of the test statistic to its sampling distribution, we can determine how likely it is to observe such a result if the null hypothesis were correct.

The key concept that arises from this comparison is the p-value. The p-value is the probability of obtaining a test statistic as extreme as, or more extreme than, the one observed, assuming the null hypothesis is true. It provides a measure of the strength of the evidence against the null hypothesis. A small p-value indicates that the observed data is unlikely under the null hypothesis and suggests that the alternative hypothesis may be more plausible. A large p-value implies that the observed data is consistent with the null hypothesis, providing little reason to reject it. The decision rule in hypothesis testing is typically to reject the null hypothesis if the p-value is less than a predetermined significance level, often denoted by alpha.

The significance level represents the maximum acceptable probability of making a Type I error, which occurs when the null hypothesis is incorrectly rejected. Common choices for alpha include 0.05, 0.01, and 0.10, depending on the context and the consequences of errors. Setting alpha at 0.05, for instance, means that we are willing to accept a 5 percent chance of rejecting the null hypothesis when it is actually true. In contrast, a Type II error occurs when the null hypothesis is not rejected even though the alternative hypothesis is true. The probability of making a Type II error is denoted by beta, and the complement, 1 minus beta, is known as the power of the test. Power measures the ability of the test to detect a true effect when one exists and depends on factors such as sample size, effect size, variability in the data, and the chosen significance level.

An essential component of hypothesis testing is the concept of the critical region or rejection region. This is the range of values for the test statistic that leads to the rejection of the null hypothesis. The boundaries of this region are determined by the significance level and the sampling distribution of the test statistic. If the observed test statistic falls within the critical region, the null hypothesis is rejected in favor of the alternative. If it falls outside, the null hypothesis is not rejected. This decision is binary and does not imply proof or certainty but rather reflects the strength of the evidence in the data.

Hypothesis tests can be one-tailed or two-tailed, depending on the form of the alternative hypothesis. A one-tailed test is used when the alternative hypothesis specifies a direction of the effect, such as whether a mean is greater than a certain value. A two-tailed test is used when the alternative hypothesis simply states that the parameter is different from the null value, without specifying the direction. Two-tailed tests are more conservative, as the critical region is split between both tails of the distribution, making it harder to reject the null hypothesis unless the observed effect is substantial.

Hypothesis testing is often misunderstood or misused, particularly when it comes to interpreting p-values. A p-value does not measure the probability that the null hypothesis is true, nor does it indicate the size or importance of an effect. It simply quantifies how surprising the data are under the assumption that the null hypothesis is correct. As such, a statistically significant result does not necessarily imply practical significance, and analysts must consider effect sizes, confidence intervals, and the broader context when interpreting results. Additionally, failing to reject the null hypothesis does not confirm it as true; it merely indicates that the data do not provide strong enough evidence to conclude otherwise.

In applied data science, the hypothesis testing framework supports a wide array of applications, from A/B testing in digital marketing to quality control in manufacturing and evaluation of scientific hypotheses in biomedical research. The framework provides a formal structure for assessing claims, guiding decisions, and ensuring that conclusions drawn from data are supported by rigorous analysis. In modern analytics environments, automated tools and statistical software carry out hypothesis tests routinely, but a deep understanding of the underlying principles is essential for correct interpretation and responsible use.

Beyond traditional parametric tests, the framework of hypothesis testing extends to nonparametric methods, permutation tests, and bootstrap-based approaches. These alternatives relax some of the assumptions required by classical tests and are especially useful when dealing with small samples, non-normal distributions, or complex dependencies. While the specific techniques may differ, the fundamental logic of comparing hypotheses, evaluating test statistics, and making decisions based on evidence remains intact.

As data grows in volume and complexity, the hypothesis testing framework continues to evolve, incorporating computational advancements and adapting to new challenges. However, its core purpose remains unchanged: to provide a disciplined, transparent, and objective means of determining whether the patterns observed in data reflect real effects or are simply the result of random variation. Understanding this framework equips data scientists and statisticians with the tools necessary to make informed judgments, reduce errors, and contribute to the advancement of knowledge through evidence-based reasoning.

Null and Alternative Hypotheses

The concepts of null and alternative hypotheses form the foundational structure of hypothesis testing, a central method in statistical inference. These two competing statements define the framework for assessing whether observed data provides sufficient evidence to support a particular claim about a population. Hypothesis testing is designed to evaluate whether patterns seen in a sample reflect actual effects in the population or whether they could simply have arisen by random chance. Understanding the role and interpretation of the null and alternative hypotheses is essential for designing sound experiments, interpreting statistical results, and making data-driven decisions across disciplines including science, medicine, economics, psychology, and engineering.

The null hypothesis, commonly denoted as H_o, represents the baseline assumption or default position. It generally proposes that there is no effect, no difference, or no relationship between the variables under investigation. For instance, if researchers are testing whether a new drug improves recovery times compared to a standard treatment, the null hypothesis would state that there is no difference in the average recovery time between the two treatments. The null hypothesis is not necessarily a statement that the researcher believes to be true; rather, it serves as a starting point for statistical analysis. The purpose of testing the null hypothesis is not to prove it true, but to determine whether the data provide strong enough evidence to reject it in favor of an alternative.

The alternative hypothesis, often denoted as H_1 or H_a, is the statement that contradicts the null hypothesis. It represents the claim that there is an effect, a difference, or a relationship present in the population. Continuing with the drug example, the alternative hypothesis might state that the new drug leads to a shorter average recovery time. Depending on the research question, the alternative hypothesis can be directional or non-directional. A directional or one-sided alternative specifies the direction of the effect, such as asserting that one mean is greater than another. A non-directional or two-sided alternative only states that there is a difference, without indicating its direction.

The formulation of null and alternative hypotheses requires careful consideration of the research context and goals. The null hypothesis should be stated in a precise and testable form, often involving equality. For example, the null hypothesis might specify that a population mean equals a certain value, or that the difference between two means is zero. The alternative hypothesis, in contrast, is usually framed as an inequality. The choice between a one-sided and a two-sided test should be made before data collection begins, based on the nature of the question being asked and the consequences of different types of errors.

One of the central features of the hypothesis testing framework is that it treats the null hypothesis as the assumption to be tested. Statistical procedures are designed to evaluate how compatible the observed data are with this assumption. If the data are highly inconsistent with what would be expected under the null hypothesis, this provides evidence against it, and the null may be rejected. If the data are consistent with the null hypothesis, then there is no strong evidence to reject it, and it is retained. It is crucial to understand that failing to reject the null hypothesis does not imply that it is true; it only suggests that there is not enough evidence in the data to support the alternative.

The logic of hypothesis testing is built around the probability of observing data as extreme as those obtained if the null hypothesis were true. This probability is known as the p-value, and it quantifies the strength of the evidence against the null hypothesis. A small p-value indicates that the observed results would be unlikely under the null hypothesis, leading to its rejection in favor of the alternative. A large p-value suggests that the observed results are not unusual, given the null, and the null hypothesis cannot be rejected. The threshold for determining whether a p-value is small enough to reject the null is called the significance level, often set at 0.05.

The formulation and interpretation of null and alternative hypotheses also play a key role in understanding statistical errors. A Type I error occurs when the null hypothesis is rejected even though it is true. This error is controlled by the significance level. A Type II error occurs when the null hypothesis is not rejected even though the alternative is true. The probability of avoiding a Type II error is known as the power of the test. The trade-off between Type I and Type II errors must be carefully managed when designing experiments and choosing test criteria.

In many practical situations, the stakes involved in making errors are high. For instance, in medical testing, rejecting the null hypothesis that a drug has no effect could lead to the approval of a new treatment, which may have wide-reaching consequences. Therefore, the formulation of the null and alternative hypotheses must be done with a clear understanding of the scientific or business context and the risks associated with different decisions. The hypotheses serve not only as statistical tools but as formalizations of the questions being asked and the claims being evaluated.

Null and alternative hypotheses also guide the design of experiments and the selection of statistical tests. The choice of sample size, the type of measurement, and the statistical method all depend on the hypotheses being tested. A well-formulated hypothesis test provides a clear benchmark for making decisions and drawing conclusions from data. Without a clear null and alternative hypothesis, statistical analysis becomes unfocused and potentially misleading.

In more complex statistical models, such as regression, analysis of variance, or machine learning, the concepts of null and alternative hypotheses continue to play a central role. In regression, for example, the null hypothesis might state that a particular coefficient equals zero, implying that the associated variable has no effect on the response. In analysis of variance, the null might assert that all group means are equal. In each case, the goal is to determine whether the observed relationships are likely to be real or merely the result of chance variation in the sample.

Formulating and interpreting null and alternative hypotheses is a foundational skill for any statistician or data scientist. It requires not only technical knowledge of statistical methods but also an understanding of the context in which those methods are applied. The hypotheses set the stage for the entire analysis, framing the question, defining the criteria for evidence, and ultimately guiding the decision-making process. Through careful construction and interpretation of null and alternative hypotheses, data analysts can turn raw observations into meaningful conclusions and contribute to the advancement of knowledge across a wide range of disciplines.

Type I and Type II Errors

In the realm of hypothesis testing, Type I and Type II errors represent two distinct ways that the testing process can lead to incorrect conclusions. These errors arise from the fundamental uncertainty involved in drawing inferences about populations based on sample data. Since the evidence from any given sample can never guarantee a definitive conclusion about the population, the risk of making errors is always present. Understanding the nature, implications, and trade-offs between Type I and Type II errors is crucial for anyone involved in statistical decision-making, as it directly affects how hypotheses are tested, how results are interpreted, and how consequences are managed in practical applications.

A Type I error occurs when a true null hypothesis is incorrectly rejected. In other words, the test concludes that there is an effect or difference when in reality none exists. This type of error is sometimes referred to as a false positive. For instance, suppose a pharmaceutical company tests a new drug to determine whether it is more effective than an existing treatment. If the statistical test rejects the null hypothesis and concludes that the new drug is superior when in fact it is not, a Type I error has been made. The risk of this error is quantified by the significance level of the test, commonly denoted by the Greek letter alpha. If a test is conducted at the 5% significance level, there is a 5% chance of rejecting the null hypothesis when it is actually true.

The choice of alpha reflects the analyst's willingness to tolerate the risk of a Type I error. In many scientific fields, the conventional standard is to set alpha at 0.05, though stricter thresholds such as 0.01 or 0.001 may be used when the consequences of a false positive are severe. For example, in clinical trials or high-stakes regulatory decisions, reducing the probability of a Type I error may be critical to ensure public safety. However, lowering alpha also has consequences, because it makes the test more conservative and increases the chance of committing a different kind of error.

That other error is the Type II error, which occurs when a false null hypothesis is not rejected. In this case, the test fails to detect an effect or difference that actually exists, leading to a false negative conclusion. For example, in the same pharmaceutical study, a Type II error would occur if the test concludes that the new drug is no better than the existing treatment when, in fact, it is more effective. The probability of a Type II error is denoted by the Greek letter beta, and the complement of beta, 1 minus beta, is known as the power of the test. Power represents the probability of correctly rejecting a false null hypothesis, and it is a key consideration in designing effective experiments and studies.

Balancing Type I and Type II errors is a fundamental challenge in hypothesis testing. Reducing the probability of one typically increases the probability of the other. If alpha is set very low to minimize the risk of Type I errors, the test may become less sensitive, increasing the risk of Type II errors. Conversely, if the test is made very sensitive to detect even small effects, the likelihood of rejecting the null hypothesis increases, but so does the chance of rejecting it when it is actually true. This trade-off means that decisions about significance levels, sample sizes, and test power must be made carefully, taking into account the context and the potential costs of each type of error.

Several factors influence the probability of making Type I and Type II errors. The sample size is one of the most important. Larger samples provide more information and reduce the variability of estimates, which enhances the ability to detect true effects and reduces the risk of both types of errors. Increasing the sample size typically increases the power of a test and allows for the use of more stringent significance levels without sacrificing sensitivity. The true effect size also plays a crucial role. Larger effect sizes are easier to detect and reduce the chance of a Type II error, while small effect sizes may be missed unless the study is carefully designed with sufficient power.

The variability of the data, reflected in the standard deviation or variance, also affects the likelihood of errors. High variability makes it harder to distinguish signal from noise, increasing the chances of both

Type I and Type II errors. Reducing variability through better measurement techniques, more consistent data collection, or controlling for confounding variables can help improve the accuracy of the test. Additionally, the choice of test statistic and testing procedure can influence error rates. Different statistical tests have different sensitivities to data characteristics such as normality, homoscedasticity, and independence, and choosing the appropriate method for the context is essential for minimizing errors.

In practice, the implications of Type I and Type II errors depend on the domain of application. In the legal system, for example, a Type I error might correspond to convicting an innocent person, while a Type II error might correspond to acquitting a guilty person. The legal standard of proof is designed to minimize the risk of convicting the innocent, reflecting a societal preference to avoid Type I errors in this context. In medical diagnostics, a Type I error might result in a false diagnosis, potentially leading to unnecessary treatments, while a Type II error might result in a missed diagnosis, delaying necessary care. Depending on the disease and the treatment options, the balance between these errors must be carefully calibrated.

In scientific research, controlling Type I errors is critical to maintaining the credibility and replicability of findings. A high rate of false positives can lead to spurious discoveries and wasted resources. However, excessive caution that results in frequent Type II errors can suppress genuine discoveries and hinder scientific progress. This tension has sparked ongoing debates about the role of p-values, the reproducibility of research, and the appropriate thresholds for statistical significance. Increasingly, researchers are encouraged to report effect sizes, confidence intervals, and the power of their tests to provide a more nuanced picture of their findings.

Ultimately, understanding Type I and Type II errors is essential for making sound statistical inferences. These concepts highlight the limits of certainty in data analysis and the need for careful planning, thoughtful decision-making, and transparent communication of results. By acknowledging and managing the risks of these errors, analysts can design better studies, interpret results more accurately, and make more informed conclusions that respect both the strengths and the limitations of statistical evidence.

P-values and Statistical Significance

P-values are central to the framework of hypothesis testing and are widely used across scientific disciplines to quantify evidence against a null hypothesis. Despite their ubiquity, they are often misunderstood or misinterpreted, which can lead to flawed conclusions and misguided decisions. A proper understanding of p-values and the concept of statistical significance is essential for any practitioner of data science or statistical analysis. These tools are not just mathematical artifacts but play a crucial role in guiding inference, shaping research outcomes, and informing policy decisions.

A p-value is defined as the probability of observing a test statistic as extreme as, or more extreme than, the one obtained from the sample data, assuming that the null hypothesis is true. It measures how incompatible the observed data are with the assumption that the null hypothesis holds. The smaller the p-value, the more surprising the data are under the null hypothesis, and the stronger the evidence against it. A large p-value suggests that the data are consistent with the null hypothesis, although it does not confirm the null as true. This probabilistic measure is used to determine whether the observed effect could reasonably be attributed to random chance or whether it is more likely to reflect a true effect in the population.

In the hypothesis testing framework, a significance level is established before conducting the test. This threshold, commonly denoted by alpha, represents the maximum acceptable probability of making a Type I error—rejecting a true null hypothesis. The most commonly used alpha level is 0.05, though more stringent levels such as 0.01 or more lenient levels like 0.10 may also be used depending on the context. When the p-value is less than or equal to alpha, the result is declared statistically significant, and the null hypothesis is rejected. When the p-value is greater than alpha, the result is not statistically significant, and the null hypothesis is not rejected.

Statistical significance, therefore, is not a measure of the truth of the hypothesis but rather an indication of how likely the observed data would be if the null hypothesis were true. It is a convention-driven decision tool, not a definitive conclusion about the presence or absence of an effect. A statistically significant result suggests that the observed effect is unlikely to be due to chance alone, but it does not quantify the magnitude or practical importance of that effect. Nor does it indicate the probability that the null or alternative hypothesis is correct, a common misconception among those unfamiliar with statistical inference.

One of the key limitations of p-values is their sensitivity to sample size. In large samples, even very small and practically unimportant effects can produce tiny p-values, leading to statistical significance. Conversely, in small samples, large and meaningful effects may not reach statistical significance due to lack of power. This dependence on sample size highlights the need to interpret p-values alongside effect sizes and confidence intervals. Effect size measures the strength or magnitude of an observed relationship, while confidence intervals provide a range of plausible values for the parameter of interest. Together, these tools offer a fuller picture of the evidence than the p-value alone.

Another issue with p-values is their variability across repeated studies. Because they are based on the data from a single sample, p-values can fluctuate substantially from one sample to another, especially when the true effect size is small or the sample is underpowered. This variability contributes to the replication crisis in some fields, where studies that initially reported statistically significant findings fail to replicate in subsequent research. Such outcomes have prompted calls for more robust statistical practices, including pre-registration of hypotheses, increased sample sizes, and the use of complementary methods like Bayesian analysis.

Despite these challenges, p-values remain a useful tool when used appropriately and interpreted cautiously. They offer a standardized way to evaluate the compatibility of data with a null hypothesis and provide a basis for statistical decision-making. To enhance their usefulness, researchers are encouraged to report exact p-values rather than simply stating whether a result is significant or not. Providing the exact p-value allows others to interpret the strength of the evidence for themselves and to apply different thresholds if desired. Moreover, it is advisable to avoid dichotomous thinking, where results are labeled as either significant or not, and instead to focus on the overall weight of the evidence.

The concept of statistical significance has also been criticized for being too rigid and for promoting arbitrary cutoffs. For example, the traditional 0.05 threshold can lead to dramatically different conclusions for p-values of 0.049 and 0.051, even though the evidence provided by both is nearly identical. Some statisticians argue for abandoning the use of fixed thresholds altogether in favor of reporting p-values, effect sizes, and confidence intervals together. This more nuanced approach recognizes that evidence exists on a continuum and that decisions should be based on the totality of the evidence rather than an arbitrary cutoff.

In many real-world applications, the consequences of statistical decisions must be considered alongside p-values. A small p-value may suggest a real effect, but if the effect has little practical significance or if the cost of acting on a false positive is high, caution is warranted. Conversely, a marginally non-significant result may still merit further investigation if the potential benefits of a true effect are substantial. This contextual perspective is especially important in domains like medicine, public health, environmental science, and economics, where statistical decisions often carry real-world consequences.

P-values also play a role in model comparison and variable selection. In regression analysis, p-values are used to test whether coefficients are significantly different from zero, indicating whether a predictor contributes meaningfully to the model. However, overreliance on p-values in model selection can lead to overfitting, particularly when many variables are tested without proper correction for multiple comparisons. Techniques such as the Bonferroni correction or the false discovery rate control help mitigate the risk of false positives in multiple testing scenarios.

Ultimately, the value of p-values and statistical significance lies not in their ability to deliver black-and-white answers but in their capacity to structure reasoning under uncertainty. They provide a formal mechanism for evaluating hypotheses, quantifying evidence, and guiding action, but they must be used with an awareness of their limitations and in conjunction with other statistical tools. When interpreted thoughtfully and integrated into a broader analytical framework, p-values can help turn data into insight and support sound, evidence-based conclusions.

Power and Sample Size Calculations

Power and sample size calculations are fundamental components of sound statistical study design. These calculations determine how likely a statistical test is to detect a true effect, assuming it exists, and how much data is needed to achieve a reliable result. In hypothesis testing, power refers to the probability of correctly rejecting a false null hypothesis. It is directly related to the probability of making a Type II error, which occurs when the test fails to identify an effect that is actually present. The complement of this error probability, known as beta, is the power of the test and is usually expressed as a percentage. High power means that the test is sensitive enough to detect meaningful effects, while low power implies a greater risk of missing real findings.

Conducting power and sample size calculations before collecting data is essential for ensuring that a study is adequately equipped to answer its research questions. Studies with insufficient power are prone to inconclusive results and are at risk of wasting time and resources. On the other hand, overpowered studies may detect statistically significant results that are practically trivial, leading to misinterpretation or overemphasis of minor effects. The goal is to find a balance, determining the smallest sample size that achieves sufficient power to detect an effect of interest at a given level of statistical significance.

Several key components influence power and sample size. The first is the significance level, commonly denoted as alpha, which defines the threshold for rejecting the null hypothesis. A typical value for alpha is 0.05, meaning that the researcher is willing to accept a 5 percent chance of making a Type I error, or falsely rejecting a true null hypothesis. Lowering alpha reduces the probability of this error but simultaneously reduces power unless the sample size is increased to compensate. This trade-off highlights the interconnectedness of the elements involved in hypothesis testing.

The second major factor is the effect size, which quantifies the magnitude of the difference or relationship the test is designed to detect. Effect size can take different forms depending on the test being used, such as the difference between two means, a correlation coefficient, or an odds ratio. Larger effect sizes are easier to detect and thus require smaller sample sizes to achieve the same level of power. Conversely, when expecting a small effect, a much larger sample is needed to distinguish the signal from the noise. Accurate estimation of the expected effect size is therefore critical in designing a study with adequate power.

The third factor is the sample size itself. Larger samples provide more information, reduce the standard error of estimates, and increase the precision of the test. This, in turn, increases the power of the test, making it more likely to detect true effects. However, increasing the sample size also raises costs and logistical complexity, so it is important to calculate the minimum sample size required to achieve the desired power level. This calculation ensures that the study is both statistically rigorous and practically feasible.

The fourth component is the variability of the data, often expressed through the standard deviation or variance. Greater variability makes it more difficult to detect differences or associations, requiring larger samples to maintain power. Reducing variability through careful measurement techniques, standardized procedures, or data transformation can improve the efficiency of the study and allow for smaller sample sizes without sacrificing statistical validity.

Power analysis typically begins by specifying the desired power level, the significance level, the expected effect size, and the variability of the data. From these inputs, the required sample size can be calculated using statistical formulas or software tools. A commonly accepted standard for power is 80 percent, meaning there is an 80 percent chance of detecting a true effect if one exists. Some studies, particularly those with high-stakes outcomes or where data collection is difficult, may aim for 90 percent power or higher to further reduce the chance of missing meaningful effects.

Different types of statistical tests require different approaches to power and sample size calculation. For instance, power analysis for comparing two means involves assumptions about the expected mean difference, standard deviation, and whether a one-tailed or two-tailed test is being used. Power analysis for regression requires information about the number of predictors, the expected size of regression coefficients, and the proportion of variance explained by the model. In each case, the goal is to ensure that the design is tailored to the specific analytic strategy being employed.

In multi-phase or adaptive studies, power and sample size calculations may be revisited and adjusted as new data becomes available. This is particularly important in clinical trials, where interim analyses may lead to early stopping for efficacy or futility. Adaptive designs require careful statistical planning to maintain the integrity of the test while allowing flexibility in sample size and analysis plans.

In survey research, stratified or clustered sampling may influence sample size requirements due to design effects. In observational studies, confounding and non-random assignment can reduce effective sample size, making careful planning even more essential. In high-dimensional settings such as genomics or machine learning, where multiple comparisons are common, power must be balanced against the risk of false discoveries, often necessitating adjustments like Bonferroni correction or false discovery rate control.

Power analysis also plays a role in the interpretation of null results. A non-significant result in a study with low power does not provide strong evidence for the null hypothesis. It may simply reflect insufficient sensitivity to detect an existing effect. Reporting the power of the test, especially in studies with null findings, helps contextualize the result and avoids overstating conclusions. Similarly, in replication studies, power analysis ensures that the replication effort has enough sensitivity to confirm or refute previous findings.

Ultimately, power and sample size calculations are not just technical exercises but crucial elements of responsible statistical practice. They ensure that studies are capable of answering the questions they pose, that resources are used effectively, and that conclusions are based on solid evidence rather than chance. These calculations force researchers to think critically about the size and importance of the effects they seek to detect, to articulate their hypotheses clearly, and to design studies that are methodologically sound and ethically justified. In the landscape of modern data science and statistical inference, where the volume of information can be overwhelming and the consequences of decisions can be significant, the disciplined application of power and sample size principles remains a cornerstone of analytical integrity.

Testing Means and Proportions

Testing means and proportions is a fundamental task in statistical inference, used to compare observed sample statistics to hypothesized population values or to evaluate differences between two or more groups. These tests form the foundation of many applications in science, business, healthcare, and policy-making, where understanding average behavior or the proportion of outcomes is essential for drawing meaningful conclusions from data. Hypothesis testing of means and proportions involves formulating null and alternative hypotheses, selecting appropriate test statistics, computing p-values, and making data-driven decisions based on pre-established significance levels. Each test serves a specific purpose and relies on assumptions about the distribution and variability of the underlying data.

When testing means, the goal is to determine whether the average value of a population parameter differs from a specified value or whether the means of two populations are equal. The one-sample t-test is used when we want to test if the sample mean significantly differs from a known or hypothesized population mean. This test is appropriate when the population standard deviation is unknown and the sample size is relatively small. The test statistic is calculated by subtracting the hypothesized mean from the sample mean and dividing by the standard error of the mean, which is the sample standard deviation divided by the square root of the sample size. The resulting t-value is then compared to the t-distribution with degrees of freedom equal to the sample size minus one. If the absolute value of the t-statistic exceeds the critical value for the chosen significance level, or if the p-value is less than the significance level, the null hypothesis is rejected, indicating that the sample provides sufficient evidence of a difference.

For large samples, or when the population standard deviation is known, the z-test can be used instead of the t-test. The z-test operates under the assumption that the sampling distribution of the sample mean is approximately normal, which is supported by the Central Limit Theorem when the sample size is sufficiently large. The logic of the test remains the same, but the test statistic is evaluated using the standard normal distribution rather than the t-distribution. The z-test is less common in practice because population standard deviations are rarely known, but it remains an important theoretical tool and is often used in introductory statistics for illustrative purposes.

When comparing the means of two independent groups, such as treatment and control groups in an experiment, the two-sample t-test is the appropriate procedure. This test evaluates whether the difference between the two sample means is statistically significant by considering the pooled or separate estimates of variance depending on whether the population variances are assumed to be equal. If the variances are equal, a pooled standard error is used; otherwise, Welch's t-test is applied, which does not assume equal variances and adjusts the degrees of freedom accordingly. This flexibility makes Welch's t-test a preferred method when the equality of variances cannot be assured. Paired t-tests are used when the same subjects are measured twice under different conditions, such as before-and-after studies, where the analysis focuses on the differences within pairs rather than between groups.

Testing proportions follows a similar structure but focuses on the probability of success in a binary outcome. A one-sample z-test for proportions is used to assess whether the observed proportion in a sample differs from a known or hypothesized population proportion. The test statistic is calculated by subtracting the hypothesized proportion from the sample proportion and dividing by the standard error, which is derived from the binomial distribution. The binomial distribution approximates a normal distribution when the sample size is large and both the expected number of successes and failures exceed five. This condition, known as the success-failure rule, ensures the validity of the normal approximation and the reliability of the test.

For comparing proportions between two independent groups, such as the proportion of success in two different treatments, the two-proportion z-test is used. This test evaluates whether the difference between the two sample proportions is statistically significant, considering the combined or pooled proportion across both groups to estimate the standard error. As with testing means, assumptions about the size and balance of the samples must be considered, and the test is most reliable when the sample sizes are large and the success-failure condition is met for both groups. When sample sizes are small or when the normal approximation is questionable, exact tests like Fisher's Exact Test or the binomial test provide more accurate inference by relying on exact probability distributions rather than asymptotic approximations.

Interpreting the results of tests on means and proportions requires attention to more than just the p-value. While statistical significance provides evidence against the null hypothesis, it does not indicate the size or importance of the effect. For instance, a very small difference in means or proportions can be statistically significant if the sample size is large, but such a difference may be irrelevant in practical terms. Therefore, effect sizes and confidence intervals should always accompany test results. Confidence intervals provide a range of plausible values for the population parameter, offering a more nuanced understanding of the uncertainty surrounding the estimate and allowing for better-informed conclusions.

Both tests on means and proportions assume independent and random sampling from the population, and violations of these assumptions can compromise the validity of the results. In clustered or dependent samples, specialized techniques must be used to account for the correlation between observations. Likewise, outliers or non-normal data distributions can affect the reliability of tests on means, making non-parametric alternatives such as the Mann-Whitney U test or the Wilcoxon signed-rank test appropriate in certain situations.

In applied data analysis, the ability to correctly test means and proportions allows researchers and decision-makers to evaluate interventions, compare groups, and draw evidence-based conclusions about the behavior of populations. Whether determining the efficacy of a new drug, assessing customer satisfaction levels, or examining differences in educational outcomes, hypothesis tests on means and proportions are essential tools. Mastery of these techniques ensures that results are not only statistically valid but also meaningful in the context of real-world questions. Understanding the assumptions, proper implementation, and careful interpretation of these tests is crucial for producing reliable and actionable insights from data.

Nonparametric Testing Approaches

Nonparametric testing approaches provide powerful alternatives to traditional parametric tests, particularly when the assumptions required for parametric methods are not met. Unlike parametric tests, which rely on specific assumptions about the underlying distribution of the data—such as normality and homogeneity of variance—nonparametric tests are more flexible and robust because they make fewer assumptions. This makes them especially useful in real-world data analysis where violations of standard assumptions are common, or where the data are ordinal, skewed, or contain outliers. Nonparametric methods are grounded in rank-based or resampling techniques that preserve the validity of statistical inference in challenging conditions.

One of the key motivations for using nonparametric tests is the presence of data that deviate significantly from a normal distribution. Many parametric tests, such as the t-test or ANOVA, assume that the sample data are drawn from normally distributed populations. When this assumption is violated, the accuracy of the results can be compromised, leading to inflated Type I error rates or reduced statistical power. Nonparametric tests address this by using the order or ranking of the data rather than their specific numerical values. This strategy eliminates the dependency on distributional shape, making the tests more robust to irregularities.

The Wilcoxon signed-rank test is a classic example of a nonparametric alternative to the one-sample or paired-sample t-test. It is used when comparing the median of a single sample to a hypothesized value or when comparing two related samples, such as measurements taken before and after an intervention. Instead of analyzing the raw values, the test ranks the absolute differences between paired observations and then evaluates whether the ranks are symmetrically distributed around zero. If the data show a consistent direction of change, the test statistic will deviate from its expected value under the null hypothesis, providing evidence of a significant difference.

For independent samples, the Mann-Whitney U test serves as a nonparametric counterpart to the two-sample t-test. It evaluates whether one of two independent samples tends to have larger values than the other, without assuming that the distributions are normally shaped or have equal variances. The test is based on ranking all the observations from both groups together and then comparing the sum of the ranks between groups. If one group consistently receives higher or lower ranks, this suggests a shift in distribution, indicating a statistically significant difference. This test is widely used in medical, psychological, and social science research when dealing with ordinal data or small samples.

The Kruskal-Wallis test is an extension of the Mann-Whitney U test for more than two independent groups. It serves as a nonparametric alternative to one-way ANOVA. Like other rank-based methods, it relies on the ranks of the data across all groups rather than the raw data themselves. The Kruskal-Wallis test determines whether at least one group differs significantly in its median from the others by comparing the sum of ranks among the groups to what would be expected under the null hypothesis of identical distributions. If the test statistic exceeds a critical value, this indicates that at least one group is significantly different, though post hoc tests are needed to determine where the differences lie.

For assessing relationships between variables, nonparametric correlation coefficients such as Spearman's rank correlation and Kendall's tau offer alternatives to Pearson's correlation coefficient. Spearman's correlation assesses the strength and direction of the monotonic relationship between two ranked variables. It is particularly useful when the relationship is not linear or when the data contain outliers. Kendall's tau is similar in purpose but uses a different ranking approach that counts the number of concordant and discordant pairs, making it more robust in some contexts. These measures allow researchers to examine associations without assuming linearity or normality.

In addition to rank-based tests, nonparametric methods also include resampling approaches like permutation tests and bootstrapping. Permutation tests involve recalculating the test statistic under all possible rearrangements of the data labels to create a distribution of the test statistic under the null hypothesis. This approach is highly flexible and can be applied to almost any test statistic, making it suitable for complex or custom hypotheses. It relies on the principle that if the null hypothesis is true, the observed arrangement of the data is no more special than any other, and any observed difference should be equally likely under random reassignment.

Bootstrapping, while not a test in itself, is a nonparametric method for estimating the sampling distribution of a statistic by repeatedly sampling with replacement from the data. This technique allows for the construction of confidence intervals and hypothesis tests without relying on traditional distributional assumptions. Bootstrapping is especially valuable in small samples or in complex models where analytical solutions are difficult to obtain. By using the empirical distribution of the resampled statistics, researchers can make inferences that are both flexible and data-driven.

While nonparametric methods are often less powerful than parametric methods when all parametric assumptions are met, their robustness in the face of assumption violations makes them a vital part of the statistician's toolkit. The loss of power is typically offset by greater validity and reliability in real-world scenarios where ideal conditions are rare. Nonparametric tests are also easy to understand and interpret, as they are based on rankings and relative positions rather than abstract model parameters. This interpretability makes them appealing in fields where transparency and clarity are critical.

Despite their advantages, nonparametric tests are not entirely assumption-free. Most still require that samples are independent and randomly drawn. Some, like the Wilcoxon signed-rank test, assume the data are symmetrically distributed about the median. Additionally, nonparametric methods can struggle with very small sample sizes or with highly tied ranks, which can complicate the computation of exact p-values. Nevertheless, their ability to deliver reliable results in the face of distributional irregularities makes them indispensable for data analysts seeking robust and interpretable conclusions.

As data become more complex and varied in structure, the importance of nonparametric testing continues to grow. In modern applications such as machine learning, bioinformatics, and real-time decision systems, data often violate the clean assumptions required by traditional parametric models. Nonparametric methods offer a way forward, allowing analysis to proceed without sacrificing rigor or reliability. By focusing on the structure and relationships inherent in the data rather than fitting them to predefined models, nonparametric approaches preserve the integrity of inference and enhance the credibility of conclusions drawn from data in diverse and unpredictable environments.

Goodness-of-Fit and Chi-Square Tests

Goodness-of-fit tests are essential tools in statistics used to evaluate whether a set of observed categorical data matches an expected distribution. These tests provide a formal mechanism for comparing the frequencies observed in sample data to the frequencies expected under a specified theoretical model. One of the most widely used goodness-of-fit tests is the chi-square test, which measures the discrepancy between observed and expected frequencies across categories. The chi-square test plays a critical role in validating models, checking distributional assumptions, and supporting hypothesis testing in a variety of fields, including genetics, marketing, social sciences, and quality control.

The core idea of a goodness-of-fit test is straightforward. Suppose a researcher has a theoretical model predicting how often different categories should occur. After collecting data, the observed frequencies in each category can be compared with the expected frequencies derived from the model. The test then evaluates whether the deviations between observed and expected counts are small enough to be attributed to random variation, or whether they are large enough to suggest that the model does not fit the data well. The null hypothesis in a goodness-of-fit test states that the observed data follow the expected distribution, while the alternative hypothesis asserts that the observed data differ significantly from the expected pattern.

The chi-square statistic is calculated by summing, over all categories, the squared differences between the observed and expected frequencies divided by the expected frequency for each category. This formula weights the squared differences by the magnitude of the expected values, ensuring that discrepancies are scaled appropriately. Larger values of the chi-square statistic indicate greater deviation from the expected distribution, providing stronger evidence against the null hypothesis. Under the null hypothesis, and provided that certain assumptions are met, the test statistic follows a chi-square distribution with degrees of freedom equal to the number of categories minus one, adjusted for any parameters estimated from the data.

Several assumptions must be satisfied for the chi-square test to be valid. First, the data must consist of counts or frequencies in mutually exclusive categories. Percentages or proportions cannot be used directly without converting them to raw counts. Second, the observations must be independent, meaning that the inclusion of one observation in a category does not affect the inclusion of another. This assumption is critical and often overlooked, especially when dealing with repeated measures or hierarchical data structures. Third, the expected frequency in each category should be sufficiently large, typically at least five, to justify the use of the chi-square distribution as an approximation for the sampling distribution of the test statistic. When expected frequencies are too small, the accuracy of the test is compromised, and alternative methods such as exact tests or Monte Carlo simulations may be more appropriate.

Goodness-of-fit tests are not limited to testing uniform distributions, where each category is expected to have the same frequency. They can be used to test any theoretical distribution, such as the binomial, Poisson, or multinomial distributions. For example, in genetics, a classic application is to test whether the observed distribution of offspring genotypes matches the expected Mendelian ratios. In such cases, the expected frequencies are determined by the theoretical probabilities derived from genetic models, and the chi-square test provides a means of evaluating whether the observed data align with these predictions.

In addition to simple goodness-of-fit tests for one categorical variable, chi-square methods extend to tests of independence and homogeneity in contingency tables. The chi-square test of independence assesses whether two categorical variables are associated by comparing the observed cell frequencies in a contingency table to the expected frequencies under the assumption of independence. If the observed frequencies differ significantly from the expected ones, this suggests that the variables are not independent. The test of homogeneity is conceptually similar but is used to compare the distribution of a categorical variable across different populations or groups. Both tests use the same chi-square statistic and require the same assumptions regarding sample size and independence.

The interpretation of the chi-square test relies on the p-value associated with the calculated statistic. A small p-value indicates that the observed distribution differs significantly from the expected distribution, leading to the rejection of the null hypothesis. However, a significant result does not indicate which categories contribute most to the discrepancy. To gain further insight, analysts often examine the residuals, which are the differences between observed and expected frequencies. Standardized residuals, in particular, allow for the identification of categories where the model fits poorly by indicating how many standard deviations the observed value is from the expected value.

Chi-square tests are advantageous because they are simple to compute and applicable in many situations involving categorical data. Their reliance on frequency counts rather than underlying parameter estimates makes them accessible and intuitive for users across disciplines. However, they also have limitations. As a nonparametric test, the chi-square test lacks the power of parametric tests under ideal conditions. It also cannot handle data measured on interval or ratio scales without categorizing them, which can lead to a loss of information. Furthermore, chi-square tests do not provide estimates of the strength of association or effect size, though measures such as Cramér's V or the contingency coefficient can be used for that purpose in contingency table analyses.

With the advent of computational tools, chi-square tests can now be conducted easily even on large and complex datasets. Software packages not only compute the test statistic and p-value but also provide diagnostic tools, residual plots, and effect size measures to aid interpretation. This accessibility has led to widespread adoption of chi-square tests in automated reporting systems, dashboards, and data analysis pipelines. Despite their simplicity, proper use of these tests still requires careful attention to assumptions, data structure, and the specific question being asked.

Goodness-of-fit and chi-square tests continue to play a central role in statistical practice. They provide a rigorous yet accessible way to evaluate how well data conform to expectations and to detect meaningful deviations that warrant further investigation. Whether confirming theoretical models, exploring associations in contingency tables, or validating simulation outputs, these tests offer a robust foundation for categorical data analysis. Their versatility and interpretability ensure that they remain an essential part of the statistical toolkit for researchers, analysts, and decision-makers working in a world increasingly driven by data.

Analysis of Variance (ANOVA)

Analysis of Variance, commonly referred to as ANOVA, is a powerful statistical technique used to compare the means of three or more groups simultaneously. Unlike the t-test, which is designed for comparing means between two groups, ANOVA extends the idea to multiple group comparisons while controlling for the inflation of Type I error that would occur if multiple t-tests were performed independently. The fundamental objective of ANOVA is to determine whether the observed differences among sample means are statistically significant or whether they could reasonably have occurred by chance alone due to sampling variability. This technique is widely applied in experimental research, clinical trials, agricultural studies, industrial testing, and many other domains where comparing group outcomes is essential for understanding treatment effects or categorical influences.

The basic principle of ANOVA is to partition the total variability in the data into components that can be attributed to different sources. Specifically, the total variation in the dependent variable is decomposed into variation between groups and variation within groups. The variation between groups captures the extent to which the group means differ from the overall mean, representing the effect of the independent variable or factor. The variation within groups reflects the natural variability of observations within each group, which is assumed to be due to random error or uncontrolled factors. By comparing these two sources of variability, ANOVA assesses whether the between-group differences are large enough, relative to the within-group variability, to be considered statistically significant.

The test statistic used in ANOVA is the F-ratio, which is calculated as the mean square between groups divided by the mean square within groups. The mean square values are derived by dividing the sum of squares by their respective degrees of freedom. The F-distribution, which the F-statistic follows under the null hypothesis, is used to determine the p-value and assess the significance of the results. A large F-value indicates that the variability between group means is greater than would be expected by chance, suggesting that at least one group mean differs significantly from the others.

ANOVA relies on several assumptions that must be reasonably satisfied for the results to be valid. The first assumption is that the observations are independent, meaning that the value of one observation does not influence another. This assumption is typically met through proper study design and random sampling. The second assumption is that the data in each group are normally distributed. While ANOVA is robust to moderate deviations from normality, especially with large sample sizes, severe violations can affect the accuracy of the test. The third assumption is the homogeneity of variances, which requires that the population variances in each group be approximately equal. When this assumption is violated, the results of the standard ANOVA can become misleading, and alternative methods such as Welch's ANOVA may be used.

There are different types of ANOVA depending on the structure of the data and the research question. One-way ANOVA involves a single independent variable with multiple levels or groups. It is used to test whether there are any statistically significant differences among the group means. For example, in a study examining the effect of three different diets on weight loss, one-way ANOVA would test whether the average weight loss differs among the three diet groups. If the overall test is significant, post hoc tests such as Tukey's HSD or Bonferroni correction are performed to identify which specific groups differ from each other.

Two-way ANOVA extends the one-way ANOVA by incorporating two independent variables. This allows for the examination of not only the individual effects of each factor but also their interaction effect. An interaction occurs when the effect of one factor depends on the level of the other factor. For instance, in a study investigating the effects of teaching method and student gender on test scores, two-way ANOVA can determine whether the teaching method affects males and females differently. The interaction term adds depth to the analysis and is crucial for understanding the complexity of real-world phenomena.

Repeated measures ANOVA is used when the same subjects are measured multiple times under different conditions or over time. This design accounts for the correlation between repeated observations from the same subject and improves statistical power by reducing within-subject variability. It is commonly used in clinical trials and psychological experiments where subjects are exposed to multiple treatments or measured across different time points. However, repeated measures ANOVA introduces additional assumptions, such as sphericity, which must be tested and corrected for using methods like the Greenhouse-Geisser or Huynh-Feldt adjustments if violated.

The results of ANOVA are typically presented in an ANOVA table, which summarizes the sources of variation, degrees of freedom, sum of squares, mean squares, F-statistic, and p-value. Interpreting this table requires understanding how the variance components are calculated and how they relate to the underlying hypothesis test. A significant F-test indicates that at least one group mean is different, but it does not identify which one. Therefore, additional analysis is usually needed to make specific comparisons between groups.

ANOVA is also closely related to linear regression, and in fact, can be viewed as a special case of the general linear model. In this framework, group membership is represented by dummy variables, and the comparison of means corresponds to testing regression coefficients. This perspective allows for the extension of ANOVA to more complex designs, including analysis of covariance (ANCOVA), multivariate analysis of variance (MANOVA), and mixed-effects models. These extensions enable the incorporation of covariates, multiple dependent variables, and hierarchical data structures, greatly expanding the applicability of ANOVA in modern data analysis.

Despite its power and versatility, ANOVA should be applied thoughtfully. The interpretation of results depends not only on statistical significance but also on the context, effect sizes, and underlying assumptions. Reporting effect sizes, such as eta-squared or partial eta-squared, helps convey the practical significance of the findings and allows for better comparison across studies. Graphical methods, such as boxplots or interaction plots, can also aid in visualizing group differences and understanding interaction effects.

In practical applications, ANOVA is widely used to test product effectiveness, compare educational interventions, analyze survey results, and evaluate process improvements. Its ability to handle multiple groups and identify meaningful differences makes it an indispensable tool in both experimental and observational research. Whether used in its simplest form or as part of a more advanced model, ANOVA continues to provide a robust framework for understanding variation and testing hypotheses in a wide variety of settings. Its enduring importance in the statistical landscape is a testament to its flexibility, interpretability, and foundational role in the science of data.

Multiple Comparisons and Adjustments

Multiple comparisons and adjustments are crucial considerations in statistical inference, particularly when conducting tests across several groups or variables simultaneously. The issue arises when a single dataset is used to test multiple hypotheses. Each individual test carries a certain probability of producing a Type I error, which is the false rejection of a true null hypothesis. When many tests are performed, the probability of making at least one Type I error increases substantially. This accumulation of error risk is known as the problem of multiple comparisons, and failing to account for it can lead to misleading conclusions and overstatement of the evidence for effects that are in fact spurious.

The more hypotheses tested, the greater the chance that at least one will appear statistically significant purely by chance. If a researcher performs twenty independent hypothesis tests at a significance level of five percent, the expected number of false positives is one. This phenomenon becomes particularly problematic in fields such as genomics, psychology, clinical trials, and social sciences, where studies often involve testing hundreds or thousands of hypotheses simultaneously. The problem also occurs in exploratory data analysis, where researchers examine many potential relationships without pre-specified hypotheses, increasing the likelihood of discovering patterns that are merely artifacts of random variability.

To address the risk of inflated error rates, statisticians employ adjustment techniques that control either the family-wise error rate or the false discovery rate. The family-wise error rate is the probability of making one or more Type I errors in a family or set of tests. One of the most widely used methods for controlling the family-wise error rate is the Bonferroni correction. This method adjusts the significance level by dividing it by the number of comparisons. For instance, if ten tests are conducted and the desired overall significance level is 0.05, each test would be evaluated at a significance level of 0.005. The Bonferroni correction is simple and conservative, ensuring a strict control over Type I errors, but it can be overly stringent and reduce statistical power, making it harder to detect true effects.

Other adjustments attempt to maintain a balance between controlling error rates and preserving power. The Holm-Bonferroni method is a stepwise procedure that is less conservative than the standard Bonferroni correction. It involves ordering the p-values from smallest to largest and comparing each one to an adjusted significance level that depends on its rank. The procedure continues until a p-value fails to meet the threshold, at which point no further rejections are made. This method is uniformly more powerful than Bonferroni while still controlling the family-wise error rate.

In many modern applications, particularly in high-dimensional data analysis, controlling the false discovery rate has become a preferred strategy. The false discovery rate is the expected proportion of false positives among the rejected hypotheses. The Benjamini-Hochberg procedure is the most commonly used method for controlling the false discovery rate. It also involves ranking the p-values and comparing each one to an increasing threshold. Unlike Bonferroni-based methods, which control the chance of any false positives, the Benjamini-Hochberg approach accepts that some false positives may occur but seeks to limit their proportion. This makes the method more powerful and suitable for exploratory research or large-scale screening studies where discovering potential signals is more important than ensuring no false alarms.

Another important context where multiple comparisons arise is in post hoc analysis following analysis of variance (ANOVA). When ANOVA indicates that at least one group mean differs significantly from the others, it does not specify which groups differ. To identify the specific pairwise differences, multiple comparison procedures such as Tukey's Honest Significant Difference test, the Scheffé method, or the Dunnett test are employed. These tests adjust for multiple comparisons to maintain the overall error rate and allow researchers to draw valid inferences about group differences without inflating the risk of Type I errors.

The need for multiple comparison adjustments also extends to confidence intervals. When constructing confidence intervals for several parameters or group differences, unadjusted intervals may give a misleading impression of precision. Simultaneous confidence intervals are adjusted to ensure that the entire set of intervals collectively has a specified confidence level. This adjustment is critical in reporting multiple estimates, especially when the intervals are used for decision-making or policy recommendations. For example, in a study comparing the effectiveness of several educational programs, simultaneous intervals help ensure that the reported differences between programs are not due to chance alone.

Software implementations of multiple comparison adjustments have made it easier to apply these methods in practice, but the interpretive burden remains on the analyst. Simply applying an adjustment mechanically does not guarantee valid conclusions. Analysts must consider the context, the goals of the study, and the relative costs of Type I and Type II errors. In confirmatory studies with a clear hypothesis and pre-specified comparisons, controlling the family-wise error rate is often appropriate. In exploratory studies where the emphasis is on generating hypotheses or identifying potential leads, controlling the false discovery rate may be more suitable.

Transparency in reporting is essential when dealing with multiple comparisons. Researchers should disclose the number of tests conducted, the method used for adjustment, and the adjusted p-values or corrected confidence intervals. This allows readers to assess the robustness of the findings and guards against selective reporting, where only significant results are presented. Selective reporting not only undermines scientific integrity but also contributes to publication bias and the reproducibility crisis that affects many areas of research.

While multiple comparison adjustments are critical for maintaining the validity of statistical inference, they do not eliminate the need for good experimental design and thoughtful analysis. Properly planning the number and type of comparisons before data collection can reduce the need for extensive corrections and improve interpretability. Preregistration of hypotheses, where researchers publicly declare their intended analyses in advance, is another strategy to mitigate the impact of multiple testing. It distinguishes between confirmatory and exploratory analyses, helping to clarify which findings are supported by strong inferential evidence and which are more tentative.

Ultimately, multiple comparisons and adjustments are about respecting the uncertainty inherent in data analysis. They remind researchers that statistical significance is not an absolute verdict but a probabilistic statement that must be interpreted in context. By applying appropriate corrections and interpreting results with caution and clarity, analysts can avoid the pitfalls of false discoveries and contribute to more reliable, replicable, and meaningful scientific knowledge. As datasets grow in size and complexity, the importance of addressing the multiple comparisons problem with rigor and transparency will only continue to increase.

Correlation and Causality

Understanding the distinction between correlation and causality is one of the most important and frequently misunderstood aspects of statistical analysis and data interpretation. Correlation refers to a statistical relationship or association between two variables. It measures the degree to which changes in one variable correspond with changes in another. A positive correlation indicates that as one variable increases, the other tends to increase as well. A negative correlation suggests that as one variable increases, the other tends to decrease. Correlation coefficients, such as Pearson's r or Spearman's rho, quantify the strength and direction of these associations, typically on a scale from -1 to 1. Values closer to the extremes indicate stronger relationships, while values near zero imply weak or no linear association.

Causality, by contrast, is a much stronger and more specific claim. It implies that changes in one variable directly cause changes in another. Establishing causality requires more than just identifying a statistical relationship. It requires evidence that the cause precedes the effect in time, that the association is not due to confounding factors, and that the observed relationship remains consistent across different conditions or populations. In experimental research, causality is typically established through randomization, control groups, and manipulation of variables, which are designed to eliminate alternative explanations for observed effects. In observational studies, however, determining causality is far more complex and often requires careful modeling, domain knowledge, and sensitivity analyses.

One of the most common errors in interpreting data is to mistake correlation for causation. This mistake can have serious consequences, especially when used to guide public policy, medical treatment, or business strategy. For example, suppose a study finds that students who eat breakfast tend to perform better on exams. A naïve interpretation might conclude that eating breakfast causes improved academic performance. However, this observed correlation might be due to other factors. Students who eat breakfast may come from households with higher socioeconomic status, better parental support, or more structured routines, all of which could contribute to better academic outcomes. Without controlling for these potential confounders, the correlation cannot be interpreted as causal.

Confounding variables are variables that influence both the independent and dependent variables, potentially creating a spurious correlation. They are a major threat to causal inference, especially in non-experimental data. For instance, in examining the correlation between ice cream sales and drowning incidents, a strong positive correlation might be observed. However, the true underlying cause of both is temperature. Warm weather leads to more ice cream consumption and more swimming, which in turn leads to more drownings. In this case, temperature is the confounding variable that explains the correlation, and no direct causal relationship exists between ice cream sales and drownings.

Another complicating factor is reverse causality, where the direction of the relationship is opposite to what was initially assumed. For example, a study might show a correlation between stress and poor sleep. While it might be tempting to conclude that stress causes poor sleep, it is also plausible that poor sleep increases stress levels. In many real-world scenarios, the causal relationship may be bidirectional, and establishing the direction requires additional evidence, such as temporal sequencing or longitudinal analysis.

There are also instances where correlations are purely coincidental. These are known as spurious correlations, and they often arise when analyzing large datasets with many variables. The more variables tested, the greater the likelihood that some of them will appear correlated simply by chance. This issue is compounded by data mining and exploratory analysis practices that fail to account for multiple comparisons. Spurious correlations may be statistically significant but have no real-world meaning or explanatory power. Visualizations, domain knowledge, and replication studies are critical in identifying and discounting such relationships.

To establish causality, researchers use several methodological approaches beyond randomized controlled trials. One common strategy is the use of statistical controls, such as regression models, that adjust for the effects of confounding variables. While regression cannot prove causality, it helps isolate the relationship between the primary variables of interest by accounting for the influence of other factors. Another approach is instrumental variable analysis, which uses external variables that affect the independent variable but not the dependent variable directly, to mimic the conditions of a randomized experiment. This method is particularly useful in economics and social sciences, where randomized experiments are often impractical or unethical.

Natural experiments and quasi-experimental designs offer additional pathways to infer causality. These methods take advantage of naturally occurring variations or policy changes that approximate random assignment. For example, a sudden change in law or policy that affects one group but not another can be used to examine the causal impact of the intervention. Difference-in-differences analysis, regression discontinuity designs, and propensity score matching are examples of techniques that fall under this umbrella. While they do not offer the same level of control as randomized experiments, they provide valuable tools for causal inference when experimentation is not feasible.

Causal inference also benefits from graphical models such as directed acyclic graphs, which provide a visual representation of assumed relationships among variables. These models help clarify the underlying assumptions and guide the choice of variables to include in analysis. They are particularly helpful in identifying potential sources of bias, such as collider bias or overadjustment, which can distort estimates of causal effects if not properly addressed.

In recent years, the use of machine learning and artificial intelligence has added new complexity to the relationship between correlation and causality. Many machine learning models are designed to maximize predictive accuracy without explicitly considering causal relationships. While these models can be highly effective at forecasting outcomes, they can also reinforce existing biases or obscure underlying causal mechanisms. Understanding the limits of predictive models and integrating causal reasoning into their design is an ongoing challenge in the intersection of statistics and data science.

Correlation is a valuable first step in identifying potential relationships, guiding further investigation, and generating hypotheses. It is often the starting point in exploratory data analysis and provides insights into patterns and associations within the data. However, moving from correlation to causation requires rigorous methods, thoughtful design, and a deep understanding of the context. It demands transparency in assumptions, careful attention to alternative explanations, and a commitment to evidence-based reasoning. In a world increasingly shaped by data-driven decisions, the ability to distinguish between correlation and causality is not only a statistical skill but a critical component of responsible and informed judgment.

Linear Regression Fundamentals

Linear regression is one of the most foundational techniques in statistical modeling and data analysis. It provides a simple yet powerful framework for understanding and quantifying relationships between variables. At its core, linear regression models the relationship between a dependent variable, also called the response or outcome, and one or more independent variables, also known as predictors or explanatory variables. The primary goal of linear regression is to predict the value of the dependent variable based on the values of the independent variables and to understand how changes in those predictors influence the outcome.

The simplest form of linear regression is simple linear regression, which involves only one independent variable. In this model, the relationship between the independent variable x and the dependent variable y is represented as a straight line described by the equation $y = \beta_0 + \beta_1 x + \varepsilon$, where β_0 is the intercept, β_1 is the slope coefficient, and ε is the error term. The intercept β_0 represents the expected value of y when x equals zero, while the slope β_1 indicates the change in y associated with a one-unit increase in x. The error term ε accounts for the variability in y that is not explained by the linear relationship with x. The parameters β_0 and β_1 are typically estimated from data using the method of least squares, which minimizes the sum of squared differences between the observed and predicted values of y.

When there are multiple independent variables, the model becomes a multiple linear regression. The general form of the equation is $y = \beta_0 + \beta_1 x_1 + \beta_2 x_2 + \ldots + \beta_\square x_\square + \varepsilon$, where each x represents a different predictor, and each β represents the corresponding coefficient. This extension allows for the modeling of more complex relationships and the assessment of the simultaneous impact of several factors on the outcome. Multiple regression is widely used in economics, healthcare, engineering, and social sciences, where outcomes are influenced by many interconnected variables.

Fitting a linear regression model involves estimating the coefficients that best represent the relationship between the predictors and the response variable. The least squares estimation method provides closed-form solutions for these coefficients in most cases. The estimated regression coefficients are interpreted as the average change in the dependent variable for a one-unit change in the corresponding independent variable, holding all other variables constant. This interpretation assumes that the model is correctly specified and that the assumptions underlying linear regression are met.

Several key assumptions underpin the validity of linear regression. The first assumption is linearity, which requires that the relationship between the dependent variable and each predictor is linear. This does not mean that the variables themselves must be linear, but that their effect on the outcome can be captured by a linear combination. The second assumption is independence, meaning that the observations are not correlated with one another. This assumption is critical in time series or clustered data, where dependencies can distort results. The third assumption is homoscedasticity, which means that the variance of the error terms is constant across all levels of the independent variables. When this assumption is violated, the standard errors of the coefficients may be biased, leading to invalid inference. The fourth assumption is normality of the error terms, particularly important for hypothesis testing and the construction of confidence intervals. Although linear regression can still provide unbiased coefficient estimates without this assumption, the associated p-values and confidence intervals may be unreliable.

Once a model is fitted, various metrics and diagnostic tools are used to assess its quality and validity. The coefficient of determination, R^2, is a commonly used measure that indicates the proportion of variability in the dependent variable explained by the model. An R^2 of 1 means the model perfectly explains the data, while an R^2 of 0 means it explains none of the variation. However, R^2 alone should not be used to judge model quality, as it can be artificially inflated by adding more predictors. Adjusted R^2 accounts for the number of predictors and provides a more accurate measure of explanatory power in multiple regression settings.

Residual analysis is essential for evaluating the assumptions of linear regression. Residuals are the differences between the observed values and the values predicted by the model. Plotting residuals against fitted values can help detect non-linearity, unequal variance, or outliers. A random scatter of residuals supports the assumptions of linearity and homoscedasticity, while patterns in the residuals may indicate problems with the model specification. Normal probability plots of residuals can be used to assess the normality assumption. High-leverage points and influential observations, which can disproportionately affect the model fit, can be identified using metrics such as Cook's distance or leverage statistics.

Multicollinearity, the presence of high correlation among independent variables, is another issue in multiple linear regression. When predictors are highly correlated, it becomes difficult to isolate the individual effect of each predictor, leading to unstable coefficient estimates and inflated standard errors. Variance inflation factors (VIFs) are commonly used to detect multicollinearity, with values above a certain threshold indicating problematic correlations. When multicollinearity is present, potential remedies include removing or combining variables, using principal component analysis, or applying regularization techniques such as ridge regression or lasso.

Linear regression is not limited to numerical predictors. Categorical variables can be included in the model by coding them as dummy variables, which take on values of zero or one to indicate category membership. This allows for the inclusion of variables such as gender, treatment group, or geographic region. Interaction terms can also be added to the model to explore whether the effect of one predictor depends on the level of another. These extensions increase the flexibility of the model and allow for more nuanced understanding of the relationships in the data.

Despite its simplicity, linear regression remains a cornerstone of statistical analysis and an essential tool in the data scientist's toolkit. It provides interpretable results, forms the basis for more advanced modeling techniques, and serves as a starting point for exploratory and confirmatory data analysis. Its assumptions, while idealized, are often reasonable approximations in many practical applications, and when they are not, diagnostic tools and alternative methods are available to address violations. Through careful modeling, validation, and interpretation, linear regression continues to offer deep insights into patterns, trends, and relationships in a wide variety of data-driven fields.

Simple Linear Regression in Practice

Simple linear regression is a practical and accessible statistical method used to explore and quantify the relationship between two continuous variables. In this model, one variable serves as the predictor or independent variable, while the other is the response or dependent variable. The core idea behind simple linear regression is to draw a straight line through a scatterplot of the data that best represents the relationship between the predictor and the response. This line is defined by a linear equation, and the goal is to estimate the parameters of that equation in a way that minimizes the discrepancy between the observed data points and the values predicted by the model.

The mathematical form of a simple linear regression model is $y = \beta_0 + \beta_1 x + \varepsilon$, where y is the dependent variable, x is the independent variable, β_0 is the intercept, β_1 is the slope, and ε represents the error term. The intercept β_0 is the expected value of y when x is zero, and the slope β_1 quantifies the change in y associated with a one-unit increase in x. The error term accounts for the random variability in y that cannot be explained by the linear relationship with x. Estimating the model involves finding the values of β_0 and β_1 that minimize the sum of the squared residuals, where a residual is the difference between the actual observed value and the value predicted by the model.

In practice, simple linear regression is widely used across disciplines. In economics, it can be used to examine the relationship between education and income. In biology, it might be applied to model the growth of a plant based on the amount of sunlight received. In environmental science, one could use it to predict pollution levels based on traffic volume. Its simplicity and interpretability make it ideal for introductory analysis and initial exploration of relationships in data before moving on to more complex models.

Implementing simple linear regression begins with data collection and visualization. A scatterplot of the two variables provides an immediate sense of whether a linear relationship is plausible. If the points tend to form a cloud that aligns roughly along a straight line, a linear model may be appropriate. If the pattern is curved, discontinuous, or has clear clusters, a linear approach may be inadequate or require transformation of variables. After verifying the appropriateness of the model through visual inspection, the next step is to fit the regression line and interpret the results.

The fitting process yields estimates for the intercept and slope, along with standard errors, t-statistics, and p-values for each coefficient. The slope coefficient is often the primary focus, as it indicates the strength and direction of the relationship between the variables. A positive slope implies a direct relationship, where increases in the independent variable correspond to increases in the dependent variable. A negative slope suggests an inverse relationship. The p-value for the slope tests the null hypothesis that there is no linear relationship between the variables, i.e., that the true slope is zero. A small p-value indicates that the relationship is statistically significant, meaning that it is unlikely to have occurred by random chance alone.

In addition to coefficient estimates, the regression output includes the R^2 value, which indicates the proportion of the variance in the dependent variable that is explained by the independent variable. An R^2 of 0.75, for example, means that 75 percent of the variation in y can be explained by the linear relationship with x, while the remaining 25 percent is due to other factors or random noise. While a high R^2 is desirable, it does not guarantee that the model is appropriate. A low R^2 does not necessarily mean the model is useless, especially in fields where a large amount of natural variability is expected.

After fitting the model, residual analysis is essential for validating the assumptions of linear regression. Residuals should be randomly scattered around zero when plotted against the predicted values or the independent variable. Patterns in the residuals, such as curves or funnels, may indicate non-linearity or heteroscedasticity, where the variance of the errors is not constant across all levels of the predictor. These violations can compromise the reliability of standard errors and hypothesis tests. If such issues are detected, data transformations, such as taking logarithms or applying polynomial terms, might be necessary to better capture the underlying relationship.

Another important practical consideration is the presence of outliers and influential points. Outliers are observations with large residuals that do not follow the general pattern of the data, while influential points have a disproportionately large effect on the estimated regression line. Diagnostic tools like leverage plots, Cook's distance, and standardized residuals help identify such points. Decisions about whether to exclude or investigate outliers should be made carefully and transparently, considering the context and the possible causes of the anomalies.

Simple linear regression can also be used for prediction, which is one of its most common applications. Once the model is fitted, it can be used to estimate the value of the dependent variable for new observations of the independent variable. Prediction intervals can be constructed to express the uncertainty around these estimates. It is important to distinguish between confidence intervals for the mean response and prediction intervals for individual responses, with the latter being wider to reflect the additional uncertainty.

While simple linear regression is a powerful tool, its utility depends on thoughtful application. Analysts must understand its assumptions and limitations, interpret the results in context, and avoid overreliance on statistical significance alone. A statistically significant slope does not imply causation, and a high R^2 does not confirm the model's validity. The choice of variables, data quality, and domain knowledge all influence the conclusions that can be drawn from a regression analysis.

In many cases, simple linear regression serves as the gateway to more sophisticated modeling techniques. Once a basic understanding of the relationship is established, analysts may incorporate additional predictors, explore interactions, or apply non-linear models to better capture complexity. However, the principles learned from simple linear regression remain fundamental. The ideas of minimizing error, interpreting coefficients, and validating assumptions carry through to more advanced methods. As such, mastering simple linear regression is not only an end in itself but a foundation for deeper statistical learning and more effective data-driven decision-making.

Interpreting Regression Coefficients

Interpreting regression coefficients is a fundamental aspect of understanding and communicating the results of a linear regression analysis. Regression coefficients provide the quantitative relationship between each predictor variable and the dependent variable, allowing analysts to make sense of how different factors contribute to the outcome of interest. The ability to interpret these coefficients accurately is essential for drawing valid conclusions, making informed decisions, and translating statistical findings into practical insights. Each coefficient in a regression model carries specific meaning, which depends on the scale of the variables, the presence of other predictors, and the structure of the model.

In a simple linear regression model with one independent variable, the interpretation of the coefficients is relatively straightforward. The intercept represents the expected value of the dependent variable when the independent variable is equal to zero. While this is a mathematically necessary component of the model, its practical relevance depends on whether a value of zero for the independent variable is meaningful in the context of the data. In many cases, the intercept is not of primary interest, especially if zero is outside the observed range of the predictor. Nevertheless, it is part of the regression equation and is necessary for making predictions.

The slope coefficient in simple linear regression represents the expected change in the dependent variable associated with a one-unit increase in the independent variable. For example, if the regression model is predicting income based on years of education, and the slope is estimated at 2,000, this suggests that each additional year of education is associated with a $2,000 increase in income, on average, assuming all other factors are held constant. This interpretation is powerful because it quantifies the strength and direction of the relationship, giving decision-makers and researchers a concrete sense of the effect size.

In multiple linear regression, where more than one predictor is included, the interpretation of each coefficient becomes conditional on the other variables in the model. Each coefficient represents the expected change in the dependent variable for a one-unit change in the corresponding predictor, holding all other predictors constant. This notion of holding other variables constant is critical because it distinguishes the unique contribution of each variable after accounting for the influence of the others. For instance, in a model predicting housing prices based on square footage, number of bedrooms, and distance to the city center, the coefficient for square footage tells us how much the price is expected to change for each additional square foot, assuming the number of bedrooms and distance to the city center remain unchanged.

The presence of multicollinearity, where predictors are highly correlated with one another, can complicate the interpretation of coefficients. When multicollinearity exists, it becomes difficult to disentangle the individual effects of the predictors because changes in one variable are associated with changes in another. This can lead to unstable coefficient estimates, inflated standard errors, and coefficients that may not reflect the true relationship between the predictors and the response variable. In such cases, even variables that have a real impact may appear statistically insignificant. Diagnostic tools like variance inflation factors help identify multicollinearity, and strategies such as variable selection, regularization, or combining correlated predictors may be used to address it.

Interpreting coefficients also requires attention to the units of measurement. A coefficient is only meaningful when the units of the variables are clearly understood. For example, if the predictor is measured in dollars, a one-unit increase corresponds to one dollar. If the predictor is measured in thousands of dollars, the same numerical coefficient implies a much larger effect. Standardizing the variables— transforming them to have a mean of zero and a standard deviation of one—allows coefficients to be interpreted in terms of standard deviations, facilitating comparisons between variables measured on different scales.

Categorical variables in regression models require special interpretation. These variables are typically included through dummy coding, where one category serves as the reference group and the others are represented by indicator variables. The coefficient for each dummy variable indicates the difference in the dependent variable between that category and the reference group. For example, in a model predicting test scores based on school type, with public schools as the reference group, the coefficient for private school might represent the average difference in scores between private and public schools, all else being equal. Understanding the reference category is crucial for making correct interpretations, as the meaning of the coefficients depends entirely on that baseline comparison.

Interaction terms in regression models introduce an additional layer of complexity. An interaction term represents the combined effect of two variables that is different from the sum of their individual effects. The coefficient for an interaction term quantifies how the effect of one variable changes depending on the level of another. Interpreting interaction coefficients requires examining the relationship in multiple dimensions and often benefits from graphical visualization or simple calculations of marginal effects. Failing to consider interactions can lead to incorrect or oversimplified conclusions, especially in cases where the effect of one variable is context-dependent.

Regression coefficients are also accompanied by standard errors, which measure the uncertainty of the estimates. Smaller standard errors indicate more precise estimates. The ratio of the coefficient to its standard error forms the basis for a t-test, which evaluates whether the coefficient is significantly different from zero. The resulting p-values help determine the statistical significance of each predictor, though they should not be interpreted in isolation. Confidence intervals provide an additional tool for interpretation, offering a range of values within which the true coefficient is likely to lie. A narrow confidence interval indicates high precision, while a wide interval suggests greater uncertainty.

Beyond statistical significance, practical or substantive significance is vital when interpreting regression coefficients. A small coefficient may be statistically significant in a large sample but may have negligible practical impact. Conversely, a large effect size that fails to reach statistical significance in a small sample may still be of interest and worthy of further investigation. Contextual knowledge and domain expertise are essential for evaluating the real-world implications of regression findings.

The interpretation of regression coefficients must also consider model fit and the possibility of omitted variable bias. If important predictors are excluded from the model, the estimated coefficients may be biased, as they may capture the effects of the missing variables. This issue underscores the importance of theory-driven model specification, robust data collection, and validation of assumptions.

Accurate interpretation of regression coefficients enables meaningful insights and supports evidence-based decision-making. It requires not only technical skill but also critical thinking, careful attention to context, and a nuanced understanding of the limitations and assumptions inherent in regression analysis. As regression continues to serve as a cornerstone of data analysis across disciplines, the ability to interpret coefficients with precision and clarity remains a key competency for analysts, researchers, and decision-makers alike.

Model Assumptions and Diagnostics

Model assumptions and diagnostics form the backbone of trustworthy statistical modeling, particularly in linear regression, where the validity of the results depends heavily on whether key assumptions are met. These assumptions provide the foundation for interpreting coefficients, assessing statistical significance, constructing confidence intervals, and making predictions. When assumptions are violated, the estimates generated by a model may be biased, inefficient, or misleading, potentially leading to erroneous conclusions. Therefore, once a regression model is fitted, it is crucial to conduct thorough diagnostic checks to verify that the assumptions hold and to make appropriate adjustments when they do not.

One of the most fundamental assumptions in linear regression is linearity. This assumption states that the relationship between the independent variables and the dependent variable is linear. In simple terms, the expected change in the response variable is proportional to changes in the predictor variable. If this assumption does not hold, the model will not accurately capture the relationship, and the resulting estimates will be biased. Linearity can be evaluated by plotting residuals against fitted values or each predictor. A random scatter of residuals around zero suggests a linear relationship, whereas systematic patterns, such as curves or waves, indicate non-linearity. In such cases, transforming the predictors, adding polynomial terms, or using non-linear models may improve model fit.

Another critical assumption is independence of errors. This means that the residuals, or the differences between observed and predicted values, should be independent of one another. This assumption is often violated in time series or panel data, where observations are collected over time or grouped in clusters. When residuals are correlated, standard errors are underestimated, leading to inflated t-statistics and incorrect p-values. One way to assess independence is through the Durbin-Watson test, which checks for autocorrelation in the residuals. If significant autocorrelation is detected, models such as autoregressive integrated moving average (ARIMA) for time series data or mixed-effects models for clustered data may be more appropriate.

Homoscedasticity, or constant variance of the residuals, is another assumption that must be validated. Under this assumption, the spread of the residuals should be roughly the same across all levels of the fitted values or predictor variables. Heteroscedasticity occurs when the variance of residuals changes with the level of the predictor, often manifesting as a fan-shaped pattern in residual plots. When heteroscedasticity is present, the efficiency of the coefficient estimates is compromised, and standard errors may be biased, affecting hypothesis tests and confidence intervals. To detect heteroscedasticity, one can use visual inspection of residual plots or formal tests like the Breusch-Pagan test or White's test. Remedies for heteroscedasticity include transforming the dependent variable, applying weighted least squares, or using robust standard errors.

Normality of residuals is another assumption that plays a role in the inferential procedures of linear regression, such as constructing confidence intervals and performing hypothesis tests. This assumption requires that the residuals follow a normal distribution. While the coefficients themselves can still be estimated without this assumption, violations can lead to inaccuracies in statistical inference. The normality of residuals can be assessed visually using a histogram or a Q-Q plot, which compares the quantiles of the residuals to those of a standard normal distribution. Significant deviations from the diagonal line in a Q-Q plot indicate non-normality. The Shapiro-Wilk or Kolmogorov-Smirnov tests can also be used to formally test for normality. When normality is violated, transformations or non-parametric methods may be necessary.

Multicollinearity is another diagnostic concern, particularly in multiple regression. It arises when two or more predictor variables are highly correlated, making it difficult to isolate their individual effects on the response variable. This issue does not violate a formal assumption of regression, but it can inflate the variances of the estimated coefficients and make them unstable and sensitive to small changes in the data. As a result, the model may produce statistically insignificant results for predictors that are, in fact, important. Multicollinearity can be diagnosed by examining the correlation matrix of the predictors or by calculating variance inflation factors. A variance inflation factor greater than ten is commonly used as a rule of thumb to indicate problematic multicollinearity. Solutions include removing redundant predictors, combining them through techniques like principal component analysis, or using regularization methods such as ridge regression or lasso.

Influential points and outliers are individual data points that have an unusually large effect on the model's estimates. While all models have some residual variation, extreme values can distort the regression line and mislead interpretation. Influential observations can be detected through diagnostic measures like Cook's distance, leverage values, and DFBETAs, each of which quantifies the influence of a data point on the overall model. Visual tools such as leverage-residual squared plots or influence plots also help identify such points. When influential points are found, it is important to examine their origin and consider whether they result from data entry errors, measurement anomalies, or genuine but rare events. Depending on the context, the analyst might decide to exclude these points, use robust regression techniques, or apply transformations to lessen their impact.

In addition to these core diagnostics, model specification is an overarching concern in regression analysis. A model that omits important variables, includes irrelevant ones, or uses incorrect functional forms will yield biased or inefficient results. Specification errors can be detected by residual analysis, testing for omitted variables, and comparing alternative models. Tools like the Ramsey RESET test can help identify misspecification by detecting non-linearity and omitted interactions. Model selection criteria such as the Akaike Information Criterion (AIC) or the Bayesian Information Criterion (BIC) can also guide the choice among competing models based on their goodness of fit and complexity.

Ultimately, diagnostics are not just mechanical steps but part of a larger process of model validation and refinement. They guide the analyst in ensuring that the model reflects the data and underlying phenomena as accurately as possible. By systematically checking assumptions, identifying violations, and applying corrective techniques, one can enhance the reliability of the model's conclusions. This practice is essential in applied research, where decisions based on statistical models can affect policy, business strategy, medical treatment, and scientific theory. A model that fits the data well and meets its assumptions provides a sound basis for inference, prediction, and understanding, while a model that ignores these principles risks misleading its users and undermining its own utility. The disciplined use of diagnostics transforms regression modeling from a routine computational task into a rigorous analytical process rooted in evidence and careful reasoning.

Residual Analysis and Model Fit

Residual analysis is a cornerstone of validating linear regression models and ensuring the reliability of their interpretations and predictions. In the context of regression analysis, a residual is defined as the difference between an observed value of the dependent variable and the corresponding value predicted by the model. These residuals encapsulate the portion of the data that the model does not explain, representing the random error or deviation from the model's predictions. Studying these residuals is crucial for diagnosing model performance, checking assumptions, and identifying areas where the model might be improved. By examining the patterns in the residuals, analysts can assess whether the model fits the data appropriately and whether the assumptions underlying the regression are reasonable.

The first step in residual analysis involves plotting residuals against the fitted values. This scatterplot helps reveal any systematic structure in the residuals that would suggest model inadequacy. If the model is well-specified and assumptions hold, the residuals should scatter randomly around zero with no apparent pattern. Such a pattern suggests that the model captures the central trend of the data and that the residuals behave like random noise. However, if the residual plot reveals a curved or funnel-shaped pattern, this suggests a violation of key regression assumptions. A curved pattern indicates non-linearity, implying that the true relationship between predictors and the response variable may not be linear. A funnel shape, where the spread of residuals increases or decreases with fitted values, points to heteroscedasticity, meaning that the variance of the residuals is not constant across observations.

Another important diagnostic plot is the normal probability plot, or Q-Q plot, which is used to assess whether the residuals follow a normal distribution. This assumption is especially important for the validity of confidence intervals and hypothesis tests in regression. In a Q-Q plot, if the residuals fall along a straight line, this indicates that the distribution of residuals is close to normal. Deviations from the line, especially at the tails, suggest departures from normality. While minor deviations may not be problematic in large samples, significant departures can affect the accuracy of inference and prediction intervals. When normality is violated, data transformations or the use of robust regression methods may be necessary to obtain reliable results.

The histogram of residuals is another tool used to evaluate the normality assumption. A symmetric bell-shaped histogram supports the normality of residuals, while skewness or heavy tails indicate potential issues. In small to moderate-sized samples, visual inspection should be supplemented with formal statistical tests such as the Shapiro-Wilk or Kolmogorov-Smirnov tests to assess normality objectively. These tests provide p-values that help determine whether the residuals deviate significantly from a normal distribution. However, it is essential to interpret these tests in the context of other diagnostics and the sample size, as they can be overly sensitive or insufficiently powered in different situations.

Assessing homoscedasticity, or constant variance of residuals, is another key aspect of model fit. A model with homoscedastic residuals will have a constant spread of errors across all levels of the independent variables. This assumption ensures that the standard errors of the regression coefficients are unbiased, which in turn ensures valid hypothesis testing. If the residual plot shows a pattern of increasing or decreasing spread, this indicates heteroscedasticity. In addition to visual inspection, tests such as the Breusch-Pagan test or White's test can formally detect non-constant variance. When heteroscedasticity is present, corrective measures such as weighted least squares or the use of robust standard errors can mitigate its impact.

Another important part of residual analysis involves identifying outliers and influential data points. An outlier is an observation with a large residual, indicating that the model does not predict it well. While some outliers are simply part of the data's natural variation, others may result from measurement errors or anomalies that need to be investigated. Influential points, in contrast, are observations that have a disproportionately large impact on the estimation of regression coefficients. These are often high-leverage points, which lie far from the center of the predictor variable space. Tools such as Cook's distance, leverage values, and DFBETAs help quantify the influence of individual observations. A Cook's distance greater than one or leverage values significantly higher than the average can signal influential data points that warrant further examination.

Model fit can also be evaluated using summary statistics such as R-squared and adjusted R-squared. R-squared represents the proportion of the variance in the dependent variable that is explained by the independent variables. While a high R-squared value indicates a good fit, it does not guarantee that the model is appropriate or that it captures the true underlying relationships. R-squared can be artificially inflated by adding more variables to the model, even if those variables do not contribute meaningfully. Adjusted R-squared compensates for the number of predictors and provides a more accurate measure of fit when comparing models with different numbers of variables.

The root mean square error (RMSE) and mean absolute error (MAE) are additional metrics used to assess the accuracy of the model's predictions. RMSE gives more weight to larger errors due to the squaring of residuals, while MAE provides a more interpretable average error magnitude. Both metrics are useful for comparing models and for evaluating how well the model performs on out-of-sample data, which is critical for predictive modeling.

Cross-validation is another powerful technique for evaluating model fit, especially in predictive contexts. By splitting the data into training and validation sets or using methods like k-fold cross-validation, analysts can assess how well the model generalizes to unseen data. Poor performance on validation data, despite good fit on the training data, indicates overfitting. This occurs when the model captures noise rather than the underlying signal, leading to poor predictive performance. Regularization techniques such as ridge regression or lasso can be employed to address overfitting by penalizing large coefficients and simplifying the model.

Residual analysis and the evaluation of model fit are iterative processes. Rarely does a model pass all diagnostic checks on the first attempt. Instead, analysts refine their models by re-expressing variables, removing or transforming outliers, addressing heteroscedasticity, and improving model specification. This cycle of fitting, checking, and refining helps ensure that the model is not only statistically sound but also substantively meaningful and useful for decision-making. A model that fits well not only predicts accurately but also enhances understanding of the data, uncovers key relationships, and guides further inquiry. The integrity and credibility of statistical conclusions hinge on this rigorous diagnostic process, which transforms raw statistical output into trustworthy knowledge.

Multivariable Regression Techniques

Multivariable regression techniques extend the capabilities of simple linear regression by allowing for the simultaneous inclusion of multiple independent variables in a single model. This extension provides a more realistic and comprehensive understanding of complex relationships in data, where multiple factors typically influence an outcome. In practice, multivariable regression is one of the most widely used tools in statistics and data science because it allows analysts to control for confounding variables, assess the unique contribution of each predictor, and make more accurate predictions. The inclusion of multiple variables enables the decomposition of the influence of each factor on the response variable while adjusting for the effects of the others, offering a deeper insight into the structure of the data.

The general form of a multivariable regression model is $y = \beta_0 + \beta_1 x_1 + \beta_2 x_2 + \dots + \beta_\square x_\square + \varepsilon$, where y represents the dependent variable, x_1 through $x_\square$ are the independent variables, β_0 is the intercept, β_1 through $\beta_\square$ are the regression coefficients, and ε is the error term. Each coefficient β_i quantifies the average change in the dependent variable for a one-unit change in the corresponding independent variable x_i, holding all other variables constant. This ability to isolate the effect of each predictor makes multivariable regression particularly valuable in observational studies, where randomization is not possible and confounding is a concern.

One of the key challenges in applying multivariable regression is variable selection. Including too few variables can lead to omitted variable bias, where the effects of important predictors are misattributed to those included in the model. Including too many variables, on the other hand, can lead to overfitting, where the model captures noise rather than the underlying signal. Overfitting reduces the model's ability to generalize to new data and can inflate the variance of coefficient estimates. Variable selection techniques, such as forward selection, backward elimination, and stepwise regression, offer systematic approaches for choosing a subset of predictors based on statistical criteria. More advanced techniques like lasso and ridge regression apply penalties to the coefficients to shrink less important variables toward zero, improving model interpretability and predictive performance.

Interaction terms are another powerful feature of multivariable regression. An interaction occurs when the effect of one variable on the dependent variable depends on the level of another variable. Including an interaction term, such as x_1*x_2, allows the model to capture these conditional effects. Interpreting interaction coefficients requires care, as they modify the main effects of the interacting variables. In many applied settings, interactions reveal important nuances, such as how a treatment might work differently across demographic groups or how environmental factors might amplify or mitigate one another's effects.

Multivariable regression also allows the inclusion of categorical variables through the use of dummy or indicator coding. A categorical variable with k levels is represented by k-1 dummy variables, with one level serving as the reference category. Each dummy variable captures the difference in the dependent variable between its category and the reference group. This approach enables the inclusion of qualitative factors such as gender, region, or education level in regression models. The interpretation of coefficients for dummy variables follows the same logic as continuous predictors but is understood relative to the baseline category.

Multicollinearity, or high correlation among independent variables, is a common issue in multivariable regression. It does not violate the assumptions of the regression model per se, but it makes it difficult to estimate the individual effects of the correlated variables. When multicollinearity is present, coefficient estimates become unstable and highly sensitive to small changes in the data. Standard errors are inflated, making it harder to detect significant effects. Diagnosing multicollinearity involves examining the correlation matrix and calculating variance inflation factors. When problematic multicollinearity is detected, analysts may consider dropping one of the correlated variables, combining them into an index, or using dimension reduction techniques like principal component analysis.

Model diagnostics remain crucial in multivariable regression. All of the key assumptions of linear regression—linearity, independence, homoscedasticity, and normality of residuals—still apply and must be checked. Residual plots, leverage statistics, Cook's distance, and Q-Q plots should be examined to detect model misspecification, influential observations, and violations of assumptions. In larger models, it is also important to consider the interpretability and plausibility of the coefficients, particularly when variables are added or removed. Each change to the model may affect the coefficients of other variables, especially if those variables are correlated.

The performance of multivariable regression models can be evaluated using measures such as adjusted R-squared, which accounts for the number of predictors and helps avoid overfitting. Information criteria such as AIC or BIC provide alternative metrics that balance model fit and complexity. For predictive purposes, cross-validation is often used to assess how well the model generalizes to new data. Splitting the data into training and validation sets or applying k-fold cross-validation helps ensure that the model performs consistently and is not simply tailored to the specific sample used for estimation.

In practical applications, multivariable regression is used to answer a wide range of questions. In healthcare, it is used to identify risk factors for disease and to adjust treatment effects for patient characteristics. In economics, it is applied to model consumer behavior, labor markets, and policy impacts. In social science, it helps researchers understand the joint influence of education, income, and environment on social outcomes. The versatility of the technique allows it to be adapted to a wide variety of data types, research designs, and analytic goals.

With the increasing availability of complex and high-dimensional data, the principles of multivariable regression continue to evolve. Modern software enables the fitting of models with many variables and the application of advanced regularization techniques. Yet, the fundamental ideas remain grounded in understanding how multiple predictors together influence a response, how to isolate individual effects, and how to assess the reliability of those effects. Mastery of multivariable regression equips analysts with the tools to build richer models, uncover deeper insights, and make better-informed decisions grounded in data. As datasets grow in size and complexity, the thoughtful application of multivariable regression will continue to be a critical skill for anyone engaged in statistical modeling and data-driven research.

Multicollinearity and Variable Selection

Multicollinearity and variable selection are critical considerations in building effective and interpretable regression models. Multicollinearity occurs when two or more independent variables in a regression model are highly correlated, making it difficult to isolate the individual effect of each predictor on the dependent variable. This phenomenon can lead to instability in the estimation of regression coefficients, inflated standard errors, and misleading significance tests. Variable selection, on the other hand, involves the process of determining which predictors should be included in the model to best explain or predict the outcome of interest. These two aspects of regression modeling are closely connected, as multicollinearity often complicates the process of selecting the right variables.

When multicollinearity is present, the estimates of the regression coefficients become sensitive to small changes in the model or the data. This sensitivity arises because the model cannot clearly distinguish the independent contribution of one variable from another. For example, if two variables move together almost perfectly across the data, the model cannot determine whether one or the other is responsible for the variation in the response variable. As a result, the coefficients may fluctuate dramatically depending on which variables are included or excluded, and their signs may even reverse. Moreover, the standard errors of the coefficients become inflated, leading to wider confidence intervals and lower t-statistics, which can mask the statistical significance of truly important variables.

Diagnosing multicollinearity involves examining the relationships among predictor variables. The correlation matrix is a basic but useful tool that shows the pairwise correlations between variables. While high correlations between two variables might indicate potential multicollinearity, more comprehensive measures are often needed. One of the most widely used diagnostics is the Variance Inflation Factor, or VIF. The VIF quantifies how much the variance of a regression coefficient is increased due to collinearity with other predictors. A VIF of 1 indicates no correlation, while values above 5 or 10 are typically used as thresholds for concern, depending on the context and the field of study. Another useful metric is the condition number, derived from the eigenvalues of the predictor matrix, which measures how close the matrix is to being singular.

Addressing multicollinearity can be approached in several ways, depending on the goals of the analysis. One common strategy is to remove one of the correlated variables, especially if it does not add substantial value to the model. However, this may not always be desirable, particularly when both variables are theoretically important or when omitting one leads to omitted variable bias. Another strategy is to combine correlated variables into a single composite variable. This approach is useful when the variables represent different aspects of the same underlying construct. Principal Component Analysis can also be used to create uncorrelated components that capture the variance in the predictors, although this comes at the cost of interpretability.

Regularization techniques such as ridge regression and lasso regression offer powerful tools for dealing with multicollinearity while performing variable selection. Ridge regression adds a penalty term to the least squares objective that shrinks the regression coefficients toward zero, effectively reducing their variance and mitigating the effects of multicollinearity. Unlike ridge regression, which shrinks coefficients but does not eliminate them, lasso regression includes a penalty that can reduce some coefficients exactly to zero, thus performing automatic variable selection. Elastic net regression combines the penalties of both ridge and lasso, offering a flexible balance between coefficient shrinkage and variable selection.

The process of variable selection is fundamental in regression modeling, not only for improving predictive accuracy but also for enhancing the interpretability of the model. Including too many variables can lead to overfitting, where the model captures random noise rather than the underlying pattern, resulting in poor performance on new data. Including too few variables, or omitting key predictors, can lead to biased estimates and an incomplete understanding of the relationships within the data. The challenge lies in finding a subset of variables that provides a good trade-off between complexity and performance.

Several systematic approaches to variable selection exist. Forward selection starts with no predictors in the model and adds them one by one based on their contribution to improving a selection criterion, typically adjusted R-squared, AIC, or BIC. Backward elimination begins with all candidate predictors and removes them one at a time, eliminating the least significant variables until the model cannot be improved further. Stepwise selection is a combination of both, adding and removing variables iteratively to optimize model fit. These procedures are easy to implement but can be unstable, especially when multicollinearity is present, as small changes in the data can lead to different models being selected.

Model selection criteria such as the Akaike Information Criterion and the Bayesian Information Criterion help guide variable selection by penalizing models with more parameters, thus balancing goodness-of-fit with parsimony. Cross-validation provides an empirical method for evaluating model performance on unseen data, helping to avoid overfitting and supporting the choice of variables that generalize well. In predictive modeling, minimizing prediction error is often the primary goal, whereas in explanatory modeling, maintaining theoretical coherence and interpretability may take precedence, even at the expense of a slightly lower predictive accuracy.

Variable selection is not purely a mechanical process; it requires judgment, domain expertise, and an understanding of the research context. Variables should not be included or excluded solely on the basis of p-values or selection algorithms. Instead, the model should reflect substantive knowledge of the relationships being studied, the plausibility of the assumptions being made, and the purpose of the analysis. Including variables that are irrelevant or serve only to improve statistical fit without adding interpretive value can undermine the clarity and usefulness of the results.

Ultimately, addressing multicollinearity and selecting appropriate variables are essential steps in building robust and meaningful regression models. By carefully diagnosing multicollinearity, applying appropriate remedial measures, and using thoughtful variable selection techniques, analysts can develop models that are both accurate and interpretable. These models provide clearer insights into the data, support sound decision-making, and contribute to the development of knowledge in both scientific and applied settings. As data become increasingly complex and high-dimensional, the ability to navigate the challenges of multicollinearity and variable selection will remain a vital skill for statisticians and data scientists alike.

Transformations and Interaction Terms

Transformations and interaction terms are two powerful techniques used in regression analysis to enhance model flexibility, address assumption violations, and uncover more complex relationships between variables. In real-world data, the relationships between predictors and the outcome are rarely strictly linear, and variable effects often depend on the levels of other variables. Standard linear regression assumes that the effect of each predictor is additive and constant across all values of other predictors, and that the response variable is linearly related to the predictors. However, these assumptions are frequently violated. To capture the intricacies of real data and make better predictions or inferences, transformations and interaction terms are introduced into regression models.

Transformations involve applying a mathematical function to one or more variables in a model to address specific issues or improve model performance. These issues may include non-linearity, heteroscedasticity, non-normality of residuals, or skewed distributions. Common transformations include the logarithmic, square root, reciprocal, and polynomial functions. For example, when a predictor exhibits a diminishing marginal effect on the response, a log transformation may be appropriate, as it compresses large values and expands small ones. If the response variable is positively skewed or exhibits exponential growth, taking the logarithm of the dependent variable can stabilize variance and approximate normality of the residuals. Square root transformations are often used for count data, while reciprocal transformations can help manage hyperbolic relationships.

Transforming variables changes the interpretation of the model coefficients. When the dependent variable is log-transformed, the coefficients represent approximate percentage changes in the response variable for a one-unit increase in the predictor. When the predictor is log-transformed, the coefficient can be interpreted as the change in the dependent variable for a proportional change in the predictor. Such interpretations are especially common in economics and finance, where elasticity and relative change are of interest. However, care must be taken to ensure that the transformed variables remain interpretable in the context of the problem. Additionally, transformations should be informed by data visualization, theory, and diagnostic checks, rather than applied indiscriminately.

Sometimes, polynomial transformations are used to capture curved relationships between a predictor and the response. Including a squared or cubic term in the regression model allows the fit to bend or curve in response to the shape of the data. For instance, a quadratic term may be used to model a situation where the effect of a variable increases up to a point and then decreases, as in the case of productivity gains from experience or the relationship between stress and performance. Higher-order polynomials must be used with caution, as they can lead to overfitting and highly sensitive estimates, particularly at the boundaries of the data. Centering the variables before creating polynomial terms can also help reduce multicollinearity between the original and transformed variables.

Interaction terms, on the other hand, allow the effect of one variable to depend on the level of another variable. This is crucial in many practical situations, as the real world is full of conditional relationships. An interaction term is created by multiplying two predictors together and including this product in the model. The presence of an interaction changes the interpretation of the main effects, as the effect of one predictor now varies with the level of the other. For example, if a regression model includes education, experience, and an interaction between education and experience, the coefficient for the interaction tells us how the effect of experience on income changes as education levels vary. If the interaction coefficient is positive, it means that more education amplifies the benefit of experience.

Interpreting interaction terms requires special attention. When an interaction is included, the coefficient of a predictor represents the effect of that variable when the other interacting variable equals zero. This means that the context in which the variable is evaluated becomes important, especially if zero is not a meaningful or typical value. Centering variables before creating interaction terms can help alleviate this issue and make the coefficients more interpretable. Graphical methods, such as plotting predicted values or marginal effects at different levels of the interacting variable, are especially helpful in understanding and communicating the nature of interactions.

Interactions can also be included between categorical and continuous variables. In this case, the interaction indicates that the slope of the continuous predictor differs across the levels of the categorical variable. For example, in a model predicting sales based on advertising spending and region, an interaction between spending and region might reveal that the effectiveness of advertising varies by geographic area. When interactions between two categorical variables are included, the model allows the effect of one category to depend on the level of another, which is especially useful in studies involving treatment groups, demographic breakdowns, or policy interventions.

Transformations and interactions are not mutually exclusive and are often used together. A transformed variable can be included in an interaction term, or interaction terms can be transformed themselves. For instance, a logarithmic transformation might be applied to both variables before creating the interaction if the relationship is expected to be multiplicative rather than additive. However, combining transformations and interactions increases the complexity of the model and requires careful interpretation and validation. The risk of overfitting also grows with each additional term, particularly in small samples or models with many predictors.

Model selection and diagnostic checks are essential when using transformations and interaction terms. Measures such as adjusted R-squared, AIC, and BIC can help compare models with and without transformations or interactions. Residual plots, partial residual plots, and component-plus-residual plots can provide visual insight into whether the model adequately captures the structure of the data. Cross-validation offers a robust way to assess how well the model generalizes to new data, helping to prevent the inclusion of unnecessary or spurious terms.

Ultimately, transformations and interaction terms enhance the flexibility of regression models, allowing analysts to better represent the complexity of relationships in the data. They bridge the gap between the simplicity of linear models and the nonlinear, conditional patterns often found in real-world phenomena. When used thoughtfully, these tools improve model accuracy, reveal deeper insights, and support more nuanced interpretations. However, they demand careful application, theoretical justification, and a strong understanding of the data and context. A regression model enriched by appropriate transformations and interactions becomes not only a more powerful predictive tool but also a more faithful representation of the underlying reality it seeks to model.

Polynomial and Nonlinear Regression

Polynomial and nonlinear regression methods are essential tools in statistical modeling when the relationship between the independent and dependent variables cannot be adequately captured by a simple straight line. While linear regression assumes a constant rate of change between the variables, many real-world phenomena exhibit curves, thresholds, plateaus, or exponential patterns that violate this assumption. In such cases, applying linear models would lead to poor predictions, misleading coefficients, and invalid inferences. Polynomial and nonlinear regression techniques provide the flexibility needed to model these complex relationships more accurately, making them indispensable in fields such as biology, economics, engineering, and environmental science.

Polynomial regression is a type of linear regression in which the relationship between the independent variable and the dependent variable is modeled as an nth-degree polynomial. Although the model includes higher powers of the independent variable, it remains linear in the parameters, meaning it can still be estimated using ordinary least squares. For instance, a quadratic regression includes terms for x and x squared, while a cubic regression adds an x cubed term. These additional terms allow the regression curve to bend and fit data with more curvature than a straight line could provide. The polynomial regression equation typically takes the form $y = \beta_0 + \beta_1 x + \beta_2 x^2 + \beta_3 x^3 + \ldots + \beta_k x^k + \varepsilon$, where ε is the error term, and the degree of the polynomial, k, determines the number of inflection points the curve can accommodate.

One of the advantages of polynomial regression is its simplicity and interpretability compared to more advanced nonlinear methods. It provides a straightforward way to account for curvature in the data without changing the estimation procedure or the underlying assumptions of linear regression. However, the inclusion of higher-degree terms introduces new complexities. As the degree of the polynomial increases, the model becomes more flexible, but it also becomes more sensitive to overfitting, particularly near the edges of the data range. A high-degree polynomial may perfectly fit the training data but perform poorly on new observations. This tendency to fit noise rather than signal makes cross-validation an essential part of polynomial model selection.

Choosing the appropriate degree for a polynomial model requires a balance between flexibility and parsimony. Adding too many polynomial terms may result in a model that captures every small fluctuation in the data, while a degree that is too low may miss important patterns. Visualization plays a key role in guiding this decision. By plotting the fitted curve against the observed data, analysts can assess whether the polynomial degree adequately captures the underlying structure without introducing unnecessary complexity. Measures such as the adjusted R-squared, AIC, and BIC can also assist in determining the optimal degree, penalizing excessive complexity while rewarding better fit.

Despite its advantages, polynomial regression has limitations. It is best suited for modeling relationships that are smooth and continuous. In situations where the relationship between variables involves abrupt changes, asymptotes, or exponential growth, polynomial terms may not be sufficient. Additionally, the presence of multicollinearity can be exacerbated by polynomial terms, especially if the predictors are not centered before generating powers. Centering the variables by subtracting the mean helps reduce the correlation among the polynomial terms and improves the stability of coefficient estimates.

Nonlinear regression extends beyond polynomial models by allowing for functions that are nonlinear in the parameters. These models can include exponential, logarithmic, logistic, and power-law relationships, among many others. In contrast to polynomial regression, nonlinear regression typically requires iterative estimation methods such as the Gauss-Newton algorithm or the Levenberg-Marquardt algorithm. These methods start with initial guesses for the parameters and use optimization techniques to minimize the sum of squared errors. Because the estimation is more complex and sensitive to starting values, nonlinear regression demands careful specification and often relies on domain knowledge to guide model formulation.

Nonlinear regression is particularly useful when the functional form of the relationship is known or strongly theorized. For example, in pharmacokinetics, drug concentration over time may follow a decay curve that is best modeled with an exponential function. In population biology, growth often follows a logistic pattern, with an initial exponential phase followed by a plateau as resources become limited. In such cases, nonlinear models provide a more accurate and theoretically justified representation of the underlying processes.

Interpreting the parameters in nonlinear regression requires an understanding of the specific functional form. Unlike linear models, where each coefficient represents the effect of a one-unit change in the predictor, the interpretation in nonlinear models is often context-dependent and varies across the range of the predictor. This complexity means that numerical summaries, partial derivatives, or graphical methods are often used to communicate the results. Confidence intervals for the parameters may also be asymmetric, reflecting the curvature of the function and the uncertainty in estimation.

Model diagnostics for nonlinear regression are similar in spirit to those for linear regression. Residual analysis is critical for checking model adequacy. Plots of residuals against fitted values should show no obvious pattern if the model is appropriate. Leverage and influence diagnostics help detect observations that disproportionately affect parameter estimates. Goodness-of-fit measures such as R-squared can be adapted to nonlinear models, although their interpretation may be less straightforward. Information criteria and cross-validation continue to play a role in model selection and validation.

One of the challenges of nonlinear regression is ensuring identifiability. A model is identifiable if the data contain enough information to estimate each parameter uniquely. Poorly specified models, especially those with too many parameters or redundant terms, may lead to convergence problems or highly unstable estimates. This is why model formulation in nonlinear regression often relies heavily on subject-matter knowledge and prior research.

With the growth of computational power and statistical software, nonlinear regression has become more accessible to analysts in various disciplines. Tools now exist to fit complex nonlinear models, assess their fit, and visualize their behavior. These tools enable the exploration of data structures that were once considered too complex for traditional regression methods. However, as with any modeling approach, the key lies in thoughtful application. A nonlinear model that fits well statistically but lacks theoretical justification can be as misleading as an oversimplified linear model.

Polynomial and nonlinear regression expand the scope of regression analysis beyond straight-line relationships. They allow for greater flexibility and precision in modeling real-world phenomena, capturing nuances that linear models cannot. At the same time, they introduce new challenges in terms of model selection, interpretation, and validation. Careful use of these techniques, guided by data exploration, theory, and diagnostic checks, can lead to more accurate models and deeper insights. Whether modeling growth curves, dose-response relationships, or economic trends, polynomial and nonlinear regression provide essential tools for understanding complex patterns in data and making informed predictions in uncertain environments.

Logistic Regression for Classification

Logistic regression is a fundamental statistical technique used for classification problems, particularly when the response variable is binary. Unlike linear regression, which models a continuous outcome, logistic regression is used when the goal is to predict whether an observation falls into one of two categories. This could involve predicting whether an email is spam or not, whether a patient has a disease or not, or whether a customer will make a purchase. The technique estimates the probability of a given outcome and classifies observations based on that probability. Logistic regression is widely used across disciplines such as medicine, marketing, finance, and social sciences because it offers both interpretability and solid predictive power.

At the heart of logistic regression lies the logistic function, also known as the sigmoid function. This function maps any real-valued number into the interval between zero and one, making it ideal for modeling probabilities. The logistic function has an S-shaped curve, starting near zero, increasing rapidly in the middle, and approaching one as the input becomes large. The model uses a linear combination of predictors to form what is known as the logit, which is then passed through the logistic function to produce the predicted probability. Mathematically, the logit is defined as the natural logarithm of the odds of the outcome, where the odds are the ratio of the probability of success to the probability of failure. The logistic regression model takes the form $\log(p / (1 - p)) = \beta_0 + \beta_1 x_1 + \beta_2 x_2 + \ldots + \beta_\square x_\square$, where p is the probability of the outcome, and the right-hand side is a linear combination of the predictors.

The coefficients in a logistic regression model have a specific interpretation. Each coefficient represents the change in the log odds of the outcome for a one-unit increase in the corresponding predictor, holding all other variables constant. To make the interpretation more intuitive, the coefficients are often exponentiated to obtain odds ratios. An odds ratio greater than one indicates that the predictor increases the likelihood of the outcome, while an odds ratio less than one suggests a negative association. For example, if the odds ratio for a particular predictor is two, this means that a one-unit increase in that predictor doubles the odds of the outcome occurring.

Logistic regression models are estimated using a method called maximum likelihood estimation. This approach finds the set of parameters that maximizes the likelihood of the observed data under the model. Unlike ordinary least squares used in linear regression, maximum likelihood does not have a closed-form solution in logistic regression, and iterative optimization algorithms such as Newton-Raphson or gradient descent are used instead. These algorithms update the parameter estimates step by step until they converge to the values that best fit the data. Once the model is fitted, predictions can be made by plugging new values of the predictors into the model and computing the resulting probability. A decision threshold, typically 0.5, is then applied to convert the probability into a class label.

Evaluating the performance of a logistic regression model involves several metrics and diagnostic tools. Accuracy, defined as the proportion of correct classifications, is a common starting point. However, accuracy alone can be misleading, especially when the classes are imbalanced. In such cases, metrics like precision, recall, and the F1 score provide a more nuanced assessment. Precision measures the proportion of positive predictions that are correct, while recall measures the proportion of actual positives that are correctly identified. The F1 score is the harmonic mean of precision and recall, offering a balance between the two. The confusion matrix provides a comprehensive summary of the model's performance by showing the counts of true positives, true negatives, false positives, and false negatives.

Another important evaluation tool is the Receiver Operating Characteristic curve, or ROC curve, which plots the true positive rate against the false positive rate at various thresholds. The area under the ROC curve, or AUC, quantifies the model's ability to discriminate between the two classes. A model with an AUC of 0.5 has no discriminative power, equivalent to random guessing, while a model with an AUC of 1.0 perfectly separates the classes. The ROC curve is particularly useful when comparing multiple models or choosing an optimal threshold that balances sensitivity and specificity.

Assumptions underlying logistic regression are different from those in linear regression. The response variable must be binary, and the observations should be independent. The model assumes a linear relationship between the log odds of the outcome and the predictors, not between the predictors and the probability itself. Multicollinearity among predictors can distort coefficient estimates, just as in linear regression, and should be checked using variance inflation factors or correlation matrices. Outliers and influential observations can also impact the stability of the model, and diagnostic measures such as Cook's distance and leverage statistics can be used to detect these points.

In practice, logistic regression can be extended in several ways to handle more complex scenarios. When the outcome variable has more than two categories, multinomial logistic regression is used. For ordinal outcomes, where the categories have a natural order, ordinal logistic regression models can be applied. When data are clustered or hierarchical, mixed-effects logistic regression incorporates random effects to account for group-level variation. Regularization techniques such as lasso and ridge regression can be added to logistic models to handle high-dimensional data and prevent overfitting.

The simplicity and interpretability of logistic regression make it a strong baseline model for classification tasks. It provides direct insight into how each predictor influences the probability of the outcome and allows for statistical inference, such as testing the significance of individual predictors using likelihood ratio tests or Wald tests. Despite the rise of more complex machine learning models, logistic regression remains a popular choice due to its balance of predictive accuracy, interpretability, and computational efficiency. It is particularly valued in fields where understanding the effect of predictors is as important as prediction itself.

Logistic regression continues to be a vital method for binary classification problems. Its foundations in probability and its ability to quantify uncertainty make it more than just a tool for prediction. It enables analysts and researchers to make meaningful inferences, test hypotheses, and derive actionable conclusions from binary outcomes. When used thoughtfully and rigorously, logistic regression can reveal patterns and relationships in data that inform decision-making and contribute to understanding in a wide range of domains.

Generalized Linear Models

Generalized linear models, often abbreviated as GLMs, are an extension of traditional linear regression that allow for modeling a wider range of response variables and relationships between the predictors and the outcome. While linear regression assumes a continuous, normally distributed response variable and a linear relationship between the mean of the response and the predictors,

GLMs provide the flexibility to model outcomes that follow distributions such as binomial, Poisson, or gamma. This broader framework encompasses several commonly used models including logistic regression, Poisson regression, and others used in cases where the classical linear model would be inappropriate or misleading.

A generalized linear model consists of three components: a random component, which specifies the probability distribution of the response variable; a systematic component, which represents the linear predictor formed by a linear combination of the independent variables; and a link function, which connects the expected value of the response variable to the linear predictor. The link function is a key element that allows GLMs to handle different types of response variables. For instance, in linear regression, the identity link is used, meaning the expected value of the response equals the linear predictor. In logistic regression, the logit link is used to relate the log odds of a binary outcome to the linear predictor. In Poisson regression, used for count data, the log link relates the logarithm of the expected count to the linear combination of predictors.

One of the strengths of the GLM framework is that it separates the choice of the distribution from the choice of the link function. This separation provides a modular structure that can be adapted to various kinds of data. For example, if the response variable is a count that increases exponentially with a predictor, the log link function makes it possible to model the relationship using a linear predictor, while the Poisson distribution accounts for the discrete nature of the response. Alternatively, a gamma distribution with a log link might be used for modeling positive continuous data that are right-skewed, such as time until failure or insurance claims.

GLMs are estimated using maximum likelihood estimation, which seeks to find the parameter values that maximize the likelihood of observing the data under the specified model. This estimation process typically requires iterative algorithms such as iteratively reweighted least squares, which approximates the maximum likelihood estimates by solving a series of weighted least squares problems. These iterations continue until convergence criteria are met, producing parameter estimates that can be used for prediction and inference. The estimation procedure also yields standard errors for the coefficients, enabling the construction of confidence intervals and the performance of hypothesis tests.

Interpreting coefficients in GLMs depends on the link function and the distribution used. In a logistic regression model, the coefficients represent the change in the log odds of the outcome per unit increase in the predictor. In a Poisson regression, the coefficients correspond to changes in the log of the expected count. For models using a log link, exponentiating the coefficients yields multiplicative effects, meaning that a one-unit increase in a predictor multiplies the expected outcome by a constant factor. These interpretations can be especially meaningful in applications such as epidemiology, where relative risks and incidence rate ratios are of interest.

Model diagnostics and validation are essential components of working with GLMs. Residuals in GLMs do not behave the same way as in linear regression, due to the different distributions of the response variable. Several types of residuals are used in this context, including deviance residuals, Pearson residuals, and standardized residuals. Deviance residuals measure the contribution of each observation to the overall deviance, a measure of model fit that compares the fitted model to a saturated model that perfectly fits the data. Plots of residuals against fitted values, leverage, or predictors can reveal problems such as outliers, nonlinearity, or overdispersion. Overdispersion occurs when the variance of the response exceeds the mean, violating the assumptions of the Poisson or binomial models. When overdispersion is detected, alternative modeling approaches such as the quasi-Poisson model or negative binomial regression may be more appropriate.

Model selection in GLMs involves comparing different models using criteria such as the Akaike Information Criterion or likelihood ratio tests. The AIC balances model fit with complexity, penalizing models that include more parameters to avoid overfitting. Likelihood ratio tests can be used to compare nested models, where one model is a special case of another, by testing whether the inclusion of additional predictors significantly improves the fit. Cross-validation is another important tool, particularly when predictive performance on new data is a primary concern.

GLMs are also a foundation for more advanced statistical techniques. Generalized estimating equations extend GLMs to correlated data such as repeated measures or clustered observations, by specifying a working correlation structure and using robust standard errors. Generalized linear mixed models incorporate random effects into the GLM framework, allowing for the modeling of both fixed and random variation, which is especially useful in hierarchical data structures. These extensions maintain the core elements of GLMs while broadening their applicability to more complex data scenarios.

In applied settings, GLMs are invaluable for analyzing non-normal data that are common in health, economics, engineering, and the social sciences. Logistic regression is used to model binary outcomes such as disease presence or voting behavior. Poisson and negative binomial regressions are applied to count data such as the number of events in a time period. Gamma and inverse Gaussian models handle skewed continuous outcomes. In each case, the GLM framework provides a coherent and flexible structure for specifying, estimating, and interpreting models suited to the nature of the data.

The generality and adaptability of GLMs make them a crucial part of the statistical modeling toolkit. By allowing different distributions and link functions, GLMs provide a way to tailor models to the specific properties of the data, leading to more accurate, interpretable, and reliable results. They bridge the gap between simple linear models and the complex reality of many datasets, offering a principled way to model outcomes that do not fit the normal distribution. Through careful specification, validation, and interpretation, generalized linear models enable analysts to unlock insights from a wide range of data types and structures.

Ridge and Lasso Regression

Ridge and Lasso regression are two of the most widely used techniques in regularized linear modeling, offering powerful solutions to the common problems encountered in standard linear regression, particularly overfitting and multicollinearity. These methods are essential tools in the data scientist's toolkit, especially when working with datasets that have a high number of predictors or features relative to the number of observations. Regularization introduces a penalty to the model's coefficients, effectively constraining them and reducing model complexity. This results in models that generalize better to new, unseen data.

Ridge regression, also known as Tikhonov regularization, modifies the least squares method by adding a penalty proportional to the square of the magnitude of the coefficients. This L_2 penalty shrinks the coefficients towards zero, but it does not set them exactly to zero. The primary effect is to reduce variance, especially in cases where predictor variables are highly correlated. In the presence of multicollinearity, ordinary least squares regression assigns wildly varying coefficients to correlated variables, which can destabilize the model. Ridge regression addresses this by distributing the influence more evenly and reducing the magnitude of coefficients, leading to more reliable and interpretable outcomes.

Lasso regression, short for Least Absolute Shrinkage and Selection Operator, differs from Ridge by using an L_1 penalty instead of L_2. The key advantage of this approach is its ability to perform feature selection by shrinking some coefficients exactly to zero. This sparsity is particularly useful in high-dimensional datasets where only a subset of variables are truly relevant. By eliminating irrelevant features, Lasso simplifies the model and can enhance its interpretability without compromising predictive performance. The trade-off is that Lasso can be unstable when variables are highly correlated, as it tends to select one variable from a group and ignore the rest, potentially discarding useful information.

Both Ridge and Lasso regression can be expressed through the same fundamental framework, where the goal is to minimize the sum of squared residuals plus a regularization term. The difference lies in the nature of the penalty. In Ridge, the penalty is the sum of squared coefficients multiplied by a tuning parameter, often denoted by lambda. In Lasso, the penalty is the sum of the absolute values of the coefficients, also multiplied by a lambda. The value of lambda determines the strength of the penalty: a higher lambda increases the penalty and leads to greater shrinkage of coefficients, while a lower lambda reduces the regularization effect, bringing the model closer to standard linear regression.

Selecting the appropriate value for lambda is crucial and is typically done using cross-validation. The goal is to find a balance between bias and variance. A very large lambda may oversimplify the model, leading to high bias and underfitting, while a very small lambda may leave the model too flexible, resulting in high variance and overfitting. Cross-validation allows for an empirical approach to determining the lambda that results in the best predictive performance on unseen data.

In practice, the choice between Ridge and Lasso depends on the specific characteristics of the dataset and the modeling objectives. If the primary concern is multicollinearity and all features are expected to have at least some influence, Ridge is often the preferred method. On the other hand, if the aim is to identify a parsimonious set of influential variables from a large feature space, Lasso becomes the more suitable option. In many cases, a hybrid approach known as Elastic Net is used, which combines both L1 and L2 penalties. This method inherits the advantages of both Ridge and Lasso, offering a flexible and robust modeling solution.

The mathematical underpinnings of Ridge and Lasso regression reveal interesting geometrical interpretations. In the coefficient space, Ridge regression's constraint corresponds to a circular region, while Lasso's corresponds to a diamond-shaped region. The corners of the diamond in Lasso encourage sparsity by promoting exact zero coefficients where the loss function touches the constraint boundary. Ridge's smooth circular constraint does not encourage sparsity in the same way, hence why Ridge retains all variables even when penalized.

Computational algorithms for solving Ridge and Lasso regressions also differ. Ridge regression has a closed-form solution, which makes it computationally efficient. Lasso, due to the non-differentiability of the L1 norm at zero, does not have a closed-form solution and typically relies on iterative optimization techniques such as coordinate descent. Despite this, modern computing power and optimized algorithms have made Lasso regression practical even for large-scale problems.

From a machine learning perspective, Ridge and Lasso are foundational elements in the broader context of model regularization. They are used not only in regression tasks but also as components in more complex algorithms such as support vector machines and neural networks, where regularization plays a critical role in preventing overfitting. The concepts introduced by Ridge and Lasso extend naturally into logistic regression and other generalized linear models, enabling regularized classification as well as regression.

Understanding when and how to use Ridge and Lasso regression requires both theoretical knowledge and practical intuition. Analysts must consider the structure of their data, the goals of the analysis, and the trade-offs between model complexity and interpretability. Through proper application of these methods, it is possible to build models that are both accurate and insightful, providing reliable predictions and a clearer understanding of the underlying relationships within the data.

Cross-Validation and Model Selection

Cross-validation is a fundamental concept in machine learning and statistical modeling, serving as a crucial mechanism for evaluating model performance and guiding the process of model selection. The core idea behind cross-validation is to estimate how well a predictive model will perform on an independent dataset, thereby enabling practitioners to make more informed decisions about which model to deploy. This approach counters the inherent risk of overfitting, where a model performs exceptionally well on training data but fails to generalize to new, unseen inputs. The process involves partitioning the available data into distinct subsets, training the model on some of these subsets, and validating it on the remaining ones. By repeating this process and averaging the results, one can obtain a more reliable estimate of the model's true predictive power.

Among the most widely used forms of cross-validation is k-fold cross-validation. In this method, the data is divided into k equal parts or folds. The model is trained on k minus one of these folds and validated on the remaining fold. This process is repeated k times, each time using a different fold as the validation set and the rest for training. The final evaluation metric is calculated by averaging the performance across all k iterations. This technique provides a robust measure of performance, particularly when compared to a single train-test split, which can yield results that are highly sensitive to how the data is divided. By using k-fold cross-validation, the model is tested on every data point exactly once, which leads to a more generalized and fair assessment.

Another variation is stratified k-fold cross-validation, which is particularly useful in classification problems where the distribution of classes might be imbalanced. Stratification ensures that each fold maintains the same class proportion as the original dataset, thereby preventing misleading performance evaluations that might occur if some folds contain a disproportionately high number of examples from a single class. This technique preserves the structure of the data and yields a more accurate estimation of how the model will perform across different segments of the population.

Leave-one-out cross-validation is a special case of k-fold cross-validation where k is equal to the number of observations in the dataset. In this approach, the model is trained on all data points except one, and the single left-out point is used for validation. This process is repeated for every data point in the dataset. Although it provides an almost unbiased estimate of the model's performance, it is computationally expensive, especially for large datasets. Nevertheless, it can be advantageous in scenarios with very limited data, where maximizing the training set size in each iteration is critical.

Cross-validation is not only used to assess model performance but also plays a central role in the process of model selection. When faced with multiple candidate models or a model with various hyperparameters, cross-validation allows for an objective comparison. By evaluating each option under the same framework and choosing the one with the best average validation score, practitioners can select models that are more likely to perform well in production. This is particularly valuable when fine-tuning parameters such as the regularization strength in Ridge or Lasso regression, the maximum depth of a decision tree, or the number of neighbors in a k-nearest neighbors algorithm. Hyperparameter tuning can be conducted systematically through grid search or randomized search, with cross-validation embedded within each step to ensure fair evaluation.

Nested cross-validation offers a more rigorous method for both model assessment and hyperparameter tuning. It involves two loops: an inner loop where hyperparameters are optimized using cross-validation on the training data, and an outer loop where the model's performance is evaluated on a separate validation set. This method provides an unbiased estimate of the model's generalization ability and guards against overfitting during the tuning process. It is especially important in research settings or when reporting model performance, as it ensures that the reported metrics are not overly optimistic.

The effectiveness of cross-validation also depends on the choice of evaluation metrics. For regression tasks, metrics such as mean squared error, mean absolute error, and R-squared are commonly used. For classification problems, metrics might include accuracy, precision, recall, F1 score, and area under the ROC curve. Choosing the right metric is crucial because it defines what aspect of performance is being optimized. For instance, in medical diagnostics, minimizing false negatives may be more critical than achieving the highest overall accuracy, which makes recall a more appropriate metric than accuracy. Cross-validation helps illuminate the trade-offs between different models and metrics, providing insights that guide better decision-making.

While cross-validation is a powerful technique, it is not without limitations. It assumes that the data is independently and identically distributed, which might not hold in time-series data or datasets with spatial dependencies. In such cases, alternative methods like time-series split or blocked cross-validation are more appropriate. These variants respect the temporal or spatial order of the data and prevent information leakage from the future into the past, which would otherwise lead to misleadingly optimistic performance estimates.

Ultimately, cross-validation fosters a disciplined approach to model development. It instills a habit of empirical evaluation rather than relying on assumptions or theoretical performance. By revealing how models behave under different conditions and across various subsets of data, it acts as a safeguard against overfitting and helps avoid the common pitfall of selecting models based solely on their training performance. Through repeated training and testing cycles, it builds confidence that the chosen model will perform reliably in real-world applications, where the stakes of poor predictions can be significant. This commitment to rigorous validation underpins the broader ethos of responsible and reproducible data science.

Bootstrapping and Resampling Techniques

Bootstrapping and resampling techniques are powerful statistical tools that enable analysts and data scientists to better understand the properties of estimators, make inferences without relying on strict assumptions, and assess the stability and reliability of models. These methods revolve around the core idea of generating multiple samples from a single dataset in order to simulate the process of sampling from the population. Instead of collecting new data, which is often expensive or impractical, resampling allows us to estimate variability, construct confidence intervals, and perform hypothesis testing using computational power rather than traditional theoretical approaches.

The bootstrap method, introduced by Bradley Efron in 1979, is among the most widely used resampling techniques. It involves repeatedly drawing samples with replacement from the observed dataset, each sample being the same size as the original. Because sampling is done with replacement, some data points may appear multiple times in a single bootstrap sample, while others may not appear at all. Each of these bootstrap samples is treated as though it were a sample from the population, and the statistic of interest—such as the mean, median, regression coefficient, or standard deviation—is calculated for each resample. After many iterations, the distribution of the statistic across all bootstrap samples provides an empirical approximation of its sampling distribution.

One of the primary advantages of bootstrapping is that it requires no assumptions about the underlying distribution of the data. Traditional methods of inference often rely on assumptions such as normality, which may not hold in practice. Bootstrapping, by contrast, adapts to the actual data, making it particularly useful in situations involving small sample sizes, non-normal distributions, or complex estimators for which analytic variance formulas are not available. Through resampling, it becomes possible to construct confidence intervals, evaluate bias, and test hypotheses in a nonparametric framework.

Resampling techniques extend beyond the bootstrap. The jackknife method is another classical approach that involves systematically leaving out one observation at a time from the dataset and recalculating the statistic of interest for each of these leave-one-out samples. This method is particularly useful for estimating bias and variance and for assessing the influence of individual observations. Although the jackknife is less computationally intensive than the bootstrap, it is also less flexible, especially in estimating more complex statistics. In contrast, the bootstrap can handle a wide range of estimators and remains effective even when the structure of the data is intricate.

Another important resampling approach is permutation testing. In this method, the labels of the data are shuffled repeatedly to create new datasets under the assumption that there is no effect or difference between groups. By comparing the observed statistic to the distribution generated by these permutations, one can compute a p-value that reflects the likelihood of obtaining such a result under the null hypothesis. Permutation tests are widely used in experimental and observational studies, offering a distribution-free way to evaluate significance while maintaining the dependence structure of the data.

Bootstrapping is also instrumental in assessing model performance and validating predictive accuracy. One common application is the use of bootstrap resampling to estimate the prediction error of a model. This involves fitting the model to each bootstrap sample and evaluating it on the out-of-bag data, which consists of observations not included in that particular resample. The out-of-bag error provides an unbiased estimate of model performance, similar in spirit to cross-validation but without requiring explicit partitioning of the dataset. This technique is particularly useful in ensemble learning methods such as bagging, where multiple models are trained on bootstrap samples and their predictions are aggregated to improve robustness and accuracy.

In machine learning and data-driven science, bootstrapping plays a key role in uncertainty estimation. Rather than relying on asymptotic theory, which assumes large sample sizes and certain regularity conditions, bootstrapping provides an empirical way to quantify variability in model predictions. For instance, by applying bootstrapping to a regression model, one can obtain confidence intervals for predicted values or for coefficients, offering deeper insight into the reliability of the model. This is particularly valuable when the data is noisy or the model is complex and nonlinear.

Despite its strengths, bootstrapping does have limitations. It relies on the assumption that the observed data is representative of the population, meaning that systematic biases in the original dataset will be replicated in the bootstrap samples. Moreover, in very small samples, bootstrapping may produce overly optimistic or unstable results, especially when estimating parameters that are sensitive to outliers or rare events. Nonetheless, when used judiciously, bootstrapping remains one of the most versatile and intuitive tools for statistical inference and model evaluation.

Resampling methods, in general, reflect a broader philosophical shift in statistics and data science, where computational techniques are increasingly used to replace analytical complexity. Rather than deriving complex formulas for each specific estimator under specific distributional assumptions, resampling leverages the data itself to simulate the behavior of estimators across hypothetical samples. This approach democratizes statistical inference, making powerful tools accessible even when theoretical analysis is infeasible.

The impact of bootstrapping and resampling is evident across a wide range of disciplines, from economics and epidemiology to genomics and artificial intelligence. Their implementation is straightforward in most statistical software, and their interpretability makes them a favorite among practitioners. By grounding statistical inference in the data at hand, these methods empower analysts to make more confident and credible conclusions, especially in the face of uncertainty, limited sample sizes, or complex modeling tasks.

Permutation Testing in Practice

Permutation testing is a nonparametric statistical method that provides a flexible and powerful approach for hypothesis testing without relying on traditional distributional assumptions. Unlike classical tests that depend on specific formulas tied to assumptions such as normality or homoscedasticity, permutation testing builds an empirical distribution of the test statistic under the null hypothesis by systematically rearranging the data. This method allows analysts and researchers to assess the likelihood of observing a result as extreme as the one obtained, purely by chance, based on the actual data. Its strength lies in its simplicity, interpretability, and broad applicability across various types of data and experimental designs.

At the heart of permutation testing is the assumption of exchangeability under the null hypothesis. This means that, if there is truly no effect or no difference between groups, then the labels or group assignments of the observations are irrelevant and could have occurred in any order. For example, in a two-sample comparison, if there is no real difference between the two groups, then the data values could be randomly shuffled between the groups without affecting the truth of the null hypothesis. The test then involves calculating the test statistic for the observed data, such as the difference in means or medians between the groups, and comparing it to the distribution of the same statistic computed from many randomly permuted datasets.

To perform a permutation test in practice, one starts by computing the observed value of a chosen test statistic on the actual data. Next, the group labels are shuffled or permuted repeatedly, and the test statistic is recalculated for each permutation. After generating a large number of such permuted statistics, one constructs an empirical distribution of values that would be expected under the null hypothesis. The p-value is then estimated as the proportion of permuted statistics that are at least as extreme as the observed one. This p-value reflects how likely it is to obtain such a result by random chance, providing evidence either for or against the null hypothesis.

The number of permutations used plays an important role in the accuracy of the test. More permutations yield a more precise approximation of the null distribution, but at a higher computational cost. In most practical scenarios, a few thousand permutations are sufficient to yield stable and reliable results. The method can be applied to a wide range of statistics, including means, medians, variances, correlations, regression coefficients, classification accuracy, and even more complex metrics in machine learning models. Its versatility makes it particularly valuable in fields where traditional parametric tests are not appropriate due to the complexity or irregularity of the data.

In real-world applications, permutation testing is frequently used in biomedical research, psychology, and genomics, where data often deviate from normality and sample sizes can be small. For example, when comparing gene expression levels between two conditions in a study with only a handful of patients, traditional t-tests may not be valid due to the violation of distributional assumptions. Permutation testing provides a valid and robust alternative by relying solely on the data at hand. Similarly, in behavioral science experiments with repeated measures or matched pairs, permutation tests can be adapted to respect the structure of the data, ensuring accurate inference without the need for complex theoretical adjustments.

Another important application of permutation testing is in evaluating the performance of machine learning models. When comparing the accuracy of two classifiers on the same test set, permutation testing can help determine whether the observed difference in accuracy is statistically significant or could have arisen by chance. By permuting the predicted labels or outcomes, one can build a null distribution of the accuracy difference and assess the strength of the evidence favoring one model over another. This is particularly useful in model benchmarking and in competitions where small differences in performance can have significant implications.

Permutation tests can also be used for feature importance in models. For instance, in random forests or other ensemble models, permutation importance is a common technique where the values of a feature are randomly shuffled, and the drop in model performance is measured. If shuffling a feature leads to a significant decrease in accuracy or increase in error, it implies that the feature is important for the model's predictions. This idea is rooted in the same principles as permutation testing and provides a practical way to interpret complex, black-box models in a statistically sound manner.

Despite its many advantages, permutation testing is not without challenges. The computational burden can be significant, especially when the dataset is large or the test statistic is complex to compute. Advances in computing, parallel processing, and efficient algorithms have mitigated some of these concerns, but resource constraints may still limit its use in certain high-dimensional settings. Additionally, the validity of the test depends critically on the assumption of exchangeability. In time-series data or spatial data, where the order or location of observations carries information, naive permutation of labels may lead to invalid results. In such cases, specialized permutation schemes that preserve the inherent structure of the data must be employed.

The implementation of permutation testing has been greatly facilitated by statistical software packages, which often include built-in functions to perform these tests with user-specified statistics. Users can customize the number of permutations, select the test statistic, and visualize the permutation distribution to better understand the evidence. This accessibility has led to a surge in the use of permutation methods across academic and industrial settings, allowing for more robust and transparent hypothesis testing in a wide variety of domains.

The practical value of permutation testing lies in its direct appeal to empirical evidence rather than theoretical approximations. It allows analysts to answer the question of significance by simulating what could have happened under the null hypothesis using the actual data, making it both intuitive and rigorous. In an era of data-driven science, where complex models and unconventional data types are increasingly common, permutation testing stands out as a method that adapts gracefully to the realities of modern analysis. By grounding inference in data rather than assumptions, it continues to provide a trustworthy and flexible approach for scientific discovery and model evaluation.

Missing Data and Imputation Strategies

Missing data is a common and often unavoidable problem in real-world datasets, posing significant challenges to statistical analysis and machine learning workflows. The presence of missing values can lead to biased estimates, reduced statistical power, and incorrect conclusions if not handled appropriately. In many cases, data collection processes are imperfect, involving human error, system failures, nonresponses, or incomplete records. Understanding the nature of missing data and adopting effective imputation strategies is essential to preserving the integrity and utility of a dataset.

There are three general mechanisms that describe how data may be missing. The first is missing completely at random, or MCAR, which occurs when the probability of a data point being missing is entirely unrelated to any observed or unobserved data. In this case, the missingness is purely random and does not introduce bias into the analysis. The second mechanism is missing at random, or MAR, where the probability of missingness may depend on observed data but not on the missing values themselves. This assumption allows for more sophisticated imputation techniques that can leverage relationships within the observed data. The third mechanism, missing not at random, or MNAR, arises when the missingness depends on the value of the missing data itself. For example, in a medical survey, patients with more severe symptoms may be less likely to respond to certain questions. Handling MNAR data is particularly difficult, as it typically requires modeling the missingness process or incorporating additional assumptions.

The simplest approach to handling missing data is deletion, where rows or columns containing missing values are removed from the analysis. While easy to implement, this method can result in substantial data loss and reduced statistical power, particularly if missingness is widespread. Deletion is only justifiable under the MCAR assumption, and even then, it can lead to inefficiencies. A more principled approach involves imputation, which seeks to fill in missing values with plausible estimates derived from the available data. Imputation maintains the structure of the dataset, allowing standard analytical methods to be applied without modification.

Mean or median imputation is one of the most basic imputation methods, where missing values in a variable are replaced with the mean or median of the observed values in that variable. This method is simple and computationally efficient, but it tends to underestimate variability and distort relationships between variables. For categorical variables, mode imputation may be used, replacing missing values with the most frequent category. These univariate approaches ignore correlations among variables and are generally suitable only for preliminary analyses or when the proportion of missing data is very low.

More sophisticated imputation strategies take into account the multivariate structure of the data. Regression imputation involves modeling the relationship between the variable with missing data and other observed variables, then using the model to predict the missing values. For example, if height is missing but age and weight are available, a regression model can be fitted using the observed height values, and then applied to predict the missing ones. While this method can capture relationships among variables, it may lead to overfitting and underestimation of uncertainty, as the imputed values are treated as known rather than estimated.

Stochastic regression imputation improves upon deterministic regression by adding a random error term to the predicted values, preserving the natural variability in the data. Another powerful approach is multiple imputation, which creates several different imputed datasets by drawing values from a distribution of plausible estimates, analyzing each dataset separately, and then combining the results using established rules. This method accounts for the uncertainty associated with the missing data and yields more robust statistical inference. Multiple imputation is widely considered the gold standard for handling MAR data and is supported by many statistical software packages.

K-nearest neighbors imputation is a nonparametric method that estimates missing values based on the values of similar observations. For each missing value, the algorithm identifies the k most similar instances using a distance metric, such as Euclidean distance, and imputes the missing value using the average or majority of the neighbors. This method captures local patterns in the data and does not rely on distributional assumptions, making it suitable for both numerical and categorical variables. However, it can be computationally intensive, especially for large datasets, and the choice of k can significantly affect the results.

In machine learning pipelines, missing data handling is an essential preprocessing step. Many modern algorithms, such as decision trees and ensemble methods, can handle missing values natively or provide mechanisms for surrogate splits. However, most linear models, support vector machines, and neural networks require complete data, making imputation a necessary step before model training. Care must be taken to avoid data leakage, particularly when imputing data before a train-test split. Imputation should always be performed within each fold of cross-validation to ensure valid performance estimates.

Beyond standard imputation techniques, deep learning and probabilistic models have introduced novel ways to handle missing data. Autoencoders can be trained to reconstruct input data, learning compact representations that can be used to impute missing values. Generative adversarial networks have also been adapted for imputation tasks, modeling complex data distributions and generating realistic imputations. Bayesian methods, such as those implemented in probabilistic programming languages, allow for principled uncertainty modeling and offer a coherent framework for inference under missing data.

Choosing the appropriate imputation strategy requires careful consideration of the missing data mechanism, the proportion and pattern of missingness, the type of variables involved, and the intended analysis. Visualizing missing data patterns, such as through heatmaps or missingness matrices, can provide valuable insights into the structure and potential dependencies in the missingness. It is also important to perform sensitivity analyses to assess how results may vary under different imputation scenarios.

Ultimately, missing data is a reality in most empirical research and data-driven applications. Treating it properly is crucial to ensure the validity and reliability of findings. By applying thoughtful and statistically sound imputation strategies, it is possible to mitigate the effects of missingness and extract meaningful insights from incomplete datasets. The goal is not to recreate the true missing values, which is often impossible, but to preserve the overall structure and relationships in the data in a way that supports valid inference and decision-making.

Outliers and Robust Estimation

Outliers are observations that deviate significantly from the majority of data points in a dataset. These atypical values can arise due to a variety of reasons, including data entry errors, measurement inaccuracies, or genuine variability in the underlying phenomena. Regardless of their origin, outliers pose a challenge to statistical analysis because they can distort standard estimates, inflate variance, and lead to misleading conclusions. In the context of modeling and inference, the presence of even a few outliers can have a disproportionately large effect on results, especially when using estimators that are not robust to such deviations.

Traditional statistical techniques, including the computation of means, variances, and least squares regression, are highly sensitive to outliers. For example, the mean is easily pulled in the direction of extreme values, which may not be representative of the majority of the data. Similarly, in linear regression, the least squares method minimizes the sum of squared residuals, making it particularly vulnerable to large deviations, since squaring amplifies the influence of extreme observations. As a result, a single outlier can significantly alter the slope and intercept of a fitted line, reducing the model's overall predictive accuracy and interpretability.

Robust estimation methods aim to mitigate the impact of outliers by using techniques that are less influenced by extreme values. These methods are designed to produce reliable parameter estimates even when the data contains anomalies or deviates from idealized assumptions. One of the most fundamental robust estimators is the median, which represents the central tendency of a dataset in a way that is unaffected by extreme values. For instance, in a dataset with values mostly clustered around ten but with one value at one hundred, the mean will be skewed upward, while the median remains closer to the true center.

In regression, robust estimators include alternatives to ordinary least squares that reduce sensitivity to outliers. One such method is least absolute deviations regression, which minimizes the sum of absolute residuals rather than squared residuals. This approach assigns equal weight to all deviations, thus limiting the influence of outliers. Another widely used method is M-estimation, which generalizes maximum likelihood estimation by applying a function to residuals that diminishes the weight of large deviations. The Huber loss function is a common choice in M-estimation, blending the behavior of squared loss for small residuals with absolute loss for larger ones. This hybrid approach provides a balance between efficiency and robustness.

The identification of outliers is a crucial step before applying robust methods. Outliers can be detected through graphical techniques such as boxplots, scatterplots, and residual plots, which reveal patterns that deviate from expected distributions or model behavior. Quantitative measures such as the Z-score or Mahalanobis distance can also be used to flag extreme observations. However, caution is necessary when labeling points as outliers. Anomalous values are not always errors; they may represent important insights, such as rare events or underlying subpopulations. Removing or downweighting such points without understanding their context can lead to oversimplified models and lost information.

In multivariate settings, the detection and treatment of outliers become more complex. A point may appear normal in each individual variable but be unusual in combination with others. Multivariate outlier detection methods consider the joint distribution of variables and often rely on distance metrics or clustering techniques to identify data points that lie far from the core data structure. Techniques such as robust principal component analysis help to uncover outliers in high-dimensional spaces by projecting data onto lower-dimensional subspaces and identifying points that do not conform to the dominant patterns.

Robust estimation is not limited to central tendency or regression. It also extends to measures of spread, correlation, and covariance. The standard deviation, like the mean, is sensitive to extreme values. Alternatives such as the median absolute deviation provide a robust measure of variability that reflects the typical distance from the median, unaffected by outliers. Similarly, robust correlation measures like Spearman's rank correlation or Kendall's tau are less influenced by non-linear relationships and extreme points than the Pearson correlation coefficient. These robust statistics offer more stable and meaningful insights when data quality is imperfect.

In the context of machine learning, robustness is increasingly recognized as essential for building reliable models. Algorithms that perform well in ideal conditions may break down when confronted with noisy or corrupted data. Robust preprocessing, outlier-resistant loss functions, and anomaly detection are key components of modern data pipelines. For example, tree-based models such as random forests are inherently more robust to outliers because their splitting criteria are based on thresholds rather than numerical minimization of residuals. Ensemble methods can also reduce the effect of anomalous observations by averaging across multiple models.

The development and application of robust methods are grounded in the concept of breakdown point, which quantifies the proportion of contaminated data an estimator can handle before yielding arbitrarily incorrect results. A high breakdown point indicates strong resistance to outliers, making such estimators preferable in uncertain or heterogeneous data environments. The trade-off, however, is that robust estimators may be less efficient when the data are clean and conform to standard assumptions. Therefore, the choice between traditional and robust methods should be informed by an understanding of the data, the goals of the analysis, and the risks associated with incorrect inference.

Outliers are not inherently problematic; their significance depends on context. In fraud detection, network security, or medical diagnostics, outliers may be the most important observations, pointing to critical events or novel phenomena. Rather than simply removing outliers, robust analysis encourages a nuanced approach that preserves the structure of the data while minimizing the influence of spurious values. Robust methods provide tools to draw valid conclusions under imperfect conditions, ensuring that statistical analyses and predictive models remain reliable, interpretable, and generalizable.

Ultimately, robust estimation serves as a safeguard in the analytical process, protecting conclusions from being derailed by anomalies. It reflects a pragmatic acknowledgment that real-world data is messy and that models must be resilient to imperfections. As data becomes more complex and varied, the importance of robustness grows, highlighting the need for methods that can deliver trustworthy insights even when the data challenges conventional expectations.

Design of Experiments

The design of experiments is a cornerstone of scientific investigation and statistical analysis, providing a structured approach to exploring cause-and-effect relationships between variables. At its core, experimental design involves planning how data will be collected in a way that ensures valid, reliable, and interpretable conclusions. By carefully controlling the conditions under which observations are made, researchers can isolate the effects of specific factors and reduce the impact of confounding influences. This level of control and structure is what distinguishes an experiment from an observational study, and it allows for stronger inferences about causality.

In any well-designed experiment, the primary goal is to determine how changes in one or more independent variables, often called factors, influence a dependent variable or outcome. This is achieved through systematic manipulation of the factors under controlled conditions, followed by measurement of the resulting changes in the response variable. Randomization is a fundamental principle in this process, ensuring that experimental units are assigned to treatment groups in an unbiased manner. Randomization helps mitigate the effects of unknown or uncontrollable sources of variability, thereby enhancing the validity of the experimental results.

Another key concept in experimental design is replication, which involves repeating the same treatment conditions on multiple experimental units. Replication increases the precision of the experiment by allowing the estimation of variability within treatments, making it possible to detect real differences between treatments that are not due to random chance. Without replication, it becomes difficult to distinguish whether observed differences in outcomes are the result of treatment effects or random variation. Replication also supports the generalizability of results by demonstrating that effects are consistent across different units or instances.

Blocking is a technique used to account for known sources of variability by grouping similar experimental units together. Within each block, treatments are randomly assigned, which controls for the variability associated with the blocking factor. This approach increases the efficiency of the experiment by reducing error variance and making treatment effects easier to detect. For example, in agricultural experiments, soil type might be a blocking factor, while in clinical trials, blocks could correspond to hospitals or patient characteristics such as age groups. Blocking enhances the interpretability of the results by ensuring that comparisons between treatments are made within more homogeneous groups.

The simplest form of experimental design is the completely randomized design, where all experimental units are randomly assigned to treatment groups without consideration of any other structure. While straightforward and easy to implement, this design is most appropriate when there is little known heterogeneity among units. When there is a need to control for specific sources of variability, more advanced designs such as randomized block designs, factorial designs, and Latin square designs come into play. Each of these approaches provides a means to address different types of experimental challenges while maintaining the principles of randomization and replication.

Factorial designs are particularly powerful in experimental research because they allow the study of multiple factors simultaneously and the assessment of interactions between them. In a full factorial design, all possible combinations of factor levels are tested, providing a comprehensive view of how the factors work together to influence the response. This contrasts with one-factor-at-a-time experiments, which can be inefficient and fail to reveal important interactions. For example, in a manufacturing process, temperature and pressure might interact in a way that influences product quality, and a factorial design would uncover such a relationship that could be missed in simpler designs.

The analysis of variance, or ANOVA, is the primary tool used to analyze data from experiments. ANOVA decomposes the total variability in the data into components attributable to different sources, such as treatment effects and random error. By comparing the mean squares associated with these sources, researchers can test whether differences among treatment means are statistically significant. The interpretation of ANOVA results depends heavily on the assumptions of the underlying model, including independence, normality, and homogeneity of variance. When these assumptions are violated, alternative methods or data transformations may be necessary to obtain valid results.

Designing experiments in the presence of constraints, such as limited resources or ethical considerations, requires careful planning and often creative solutions. Fractional factorial designs are one such strategy, allowing researchers to study a subset of all possible factor combinations while still gaining valuable information about main effects and some interactions. These designs reduce the number of experimental runs needed and are particularly useful in screening experiments, where the goal is to identify the most influential factors from a larger set. Taguchi methods and response surface methodologies extend this idea further by optimizing the process through sequential experimentation and modeling of the response surface.

In modern applications, the principles of experimental design extend beyond traditional laboratory settings. In online environments, A/B testing applies experimental principles to compare two versions of a website, feature, or algorithm by randomly assigning users to different groups and measuring their behavior. Similarly, in industrial settings, design of experiments is used to optimize processes, improve quality, and reduce variability through systematic experimentation. In these contexts, the ability to draw valid causal inferences and make data-driven decisions depends on adherence to sound experimental principles.

Ethics also play an important role in experimental design, especially in fields involving human or animal subjects. Ethical experimental design requires informed consent, minimization of harm, and adherence to regulatory standards. The design must balance the pursuit of knowledge with the obligation to protect participants' rights and well-being. Institutional review boards and ethics committees review experimental protocols to ensure that these standards are met, particularly in randomized controlled trials and interventions with potential risks.

The effectiveness of an experiment depends not only on the theoretical soundness of its design but also on practical execution. Careful attention must be paid to implementation details such as measurement accuracy, consistency in treatment application, and maintenance of blinding when applicable. Even the most elegant design can be undermined by poor execution, leading to biased or inconclusive results. Therefore, successful experimentation requires collaboration among statisticians, domain experts, and practitioners to align technical rigor with real-world feasibility.

Design of experiments is ultimately about making the most efficient use of available resources to extract meaningful knowledge. By applying principles such as randomization, replication, and blocking, and by selecting appropriate design structures based on the research question and constraints, researchers can obtain clear, valid, and actionable insights. The legacy of experimental design is deeply embedded in the scientific method, and its continued relevance spans disciplines, from agriculture and medicine to engineering, psychology, and data science. The thoughtful design of experiments not only enhances the credibility of findings but also drives innovation through discovery and empirical understanding.

Randomization and Blocking

Randomization and blocking are foundational techniques in the design of experiments, serving as essential tools for reducing bias and controlling variability in empirical research. These methods are not merely procedural steps but critical elements that ensure the validity, reliability, and interpretability of experimental outcomes. When properly implemented, randomization and blocking enhance the credibility of causal inferences by mitigating the effects of confounding variables and balancing unobserved sources of variation across treatment groups. Their combined use allows researchers to isolate treatment effects with greater precision and to make robust generalizations about the phenomena under study.

Randomization refers to the process of assigning experimental units to treatment groups purely by chance. This random allocation serves multiple purposes. Primarily, it eliminates selection bias, which can occur when the assignment of treatments is influenced by subjective judgment or systematic factors. By allowing chance to determine group membership, randomization ensures that, on average, the treatment groups are equivalent in all respects except for the treatments they receive. This equivalence applies not only to observed covariates but also to unmeasured or unknown variables that might otherwise confound the relationship between the independent and dependent variables. As a result, any observed differences in outcomes can more confidently be attributed to the treatments themselves rather than to extraneous factors.

The statistical implications of randomization are profound. It justifies the use of probability theory in the analysis of experimental results and underlies the validity of many inferential procedures, including t-tests and analysis of variance. In a randomized experiment, the distribution of potential outcomes is known under the null hypothesis, allowing researchers to calculate p-values and confidence intervals with known properties. This formal connection between experimental design and statistical inference is a key advantage of randomized studies over observational ones, where causal interpretations often rely on untestable assumptions.

Despite its theoretical elegance, pure randomization may not always suffice in practice, especially when the experimental units are heterogeneous. Natural variability among subjects, environmental conditions, or measurement instruments can introduce noise into the data, obscuring treatment effects and reducing statistical power. In such cases, blocking is used as a complementary strategy to control for known sources of variability. Blocking involves grouping similar experimental units into blocks, within which treatments are randomly assigned. By comparing treatments within blocks rather than across the entire sample, the influence of block-level variability is effectively removed from the error term, leading to more precise estimates of treatment effects.

The choice of blocking factor depends on the context of the experiment and the characteristics of the units. For instance, in agricultural studies, blocks might correspond to different fields or plots with varying soil quality. In clinical trials, blocks could represent different hospitals, age groups, or disease severity levels. The aim is to create blocks that are internally homogeneous but differ from one another in ways that are not of primary interest. Within each block, treatments are randomized to prevent bias, while the blocking itself serves to reduce variability and enhance the detectability of real effects.

In the statistical analysis of blocked experiments, the variability due to blocks is accounted for explicitly in the model. This approach partitions the total variance into components attributable to blocks, treatments, and residual error. By reducing the unexplained variance, blocking increases the sensitivity of the experiment to detect true differences among treatments. This is particularly important in settings where resources are limited, and maximizing the efficiency of each experimental run is essential. Blocking also contributes to fairness in comparisons, ensuring that treatments are evaluated under comparable conditions and not unduly favored or penalized by external factors.

Randomization and blocking are often used together in complex experimental designs. For example, in a randomized complete block design, each block contains all treatments, and treatment assignments are randomized within each block. This structure is efficient and easy to analyze, providing both the benefits of randomization and the variance reduction of blocking. In other settings, more elaborate designs such as Latin squares or split-plot designs may be employed to address multiple sources of variation and logistical constraints simultaneously. These designs demonstrate the flexibility of randomization and blocking as principles that can be adapted to a wide range of experimental situations.

Practical implementation of randomization and blocking requires careful planning and attention to detail. Random number generators, randomization software, or physical devices like dice or shuffled cards can be used to assign treatments. The randomization process should be documented and reproducible, ensuring transparency and accountability in the conduct of the experiment. Similarly, the formation of blocks must be based on sound reasoning and empirical knowledge, as inappropriate blocking can introduce bias or reduce efficiency rather than improve it. Researchers must strike a balance between controlling known sources of variation and maintaining the integrity of the randomization process.

The effectiveness of randomization and blocking can be evaluated through diagnostic checks and exploratory data analysis. For instance, balance checks can verify whether covariates are evenly distributed across treatment groups, while residual plots can reveal whether blocking has successfully captured systematic patterns in the data. If imbalances or anomalies are detected, sensitivity analyses can be conducted to assess the robustness of the results to potential violations of the assumptions. These steps are crucial for ensuring that the benefits of randomization and blocking are realized in practice, not just in theory.

Beyond traditional experimental contexts, the principles of randomization and blocking have found applications in modern fields such as machine learning, online experimentation, and adaptive clinical trials. In A/B testing, users are randomly assigned to different versions of a website or application, and blocking may be used to control for factors such as geographic location or device type. In machine learning, cross-validation can be viewed as a form of blocking, where data is partitioned into folds to control for variability in model performance. These examples illustrate the enduring relevance and versatility of randomization and blocking in an increasingly data-driven world.

The integration of randomization and blocking into the design and analysis of experiments reflects a commitment to rigor, transparency, and efficiency. These techniques empower researchers to draw credible inferences from data, even in the face of complexity and uncertainty. By carefully managing variability and ensuring fair comparisons, randomization and blocking lay the foundation for trustworthy scientific conclusions and informed decision-making. Their thoughtful application is a hallmark of sound experimental practice and a key contributor to the advancement of knowledge across disciplines.

Time Series and Autocorrelation

Time series analysis is a critical area of statistics and data science focused on understanding, modeling, and forecasting data that is collected over time. Unlike traditional datasets where observations are assumed to be independent of each other, time series data exhibits temporal dependence, meaning that values are likely to be correlated with their own past and future values. This unique characteristic introduces both challenges and opportunities for analysis, requiring specialized techniques that account for the ordering and structure inherent in the data. One of the most important concepts in time series analysis is autocorrelation, which refers to the correlation of a signal with a delayed copy of itself. Recognizing and appropriately modeling autocorrelation is essential for extracting meaningful patterns and generating accurate forecasts from time-dependent data.

Autocorrelation, sometimes called serial correlation, quantifies the degree to which current values in a time series are related to past values. A positive autocorrelation indicates that high values tend to follow high values and low values tend to follow low values, suggesting a persistent pattern in the data. Negative autocorrelation, on the other hand, implies that high values are likely to be followed by low values and vice versa, reflecting a more oscillating behavior. The presence of autocorrelation violates the assumption of independence that underlies many classical statistical methods, such as linear regression, and can lead to misleading inferences if not properly addressed. Understanding the structure and strength of autocorrelation is thus a foundational step in time series analysis.

One of the primary tools for identifying autocorrelation is the autocorrelation function, or ACF, which measures the correlation between the time series and lagged versions of itself at different time intervals. By plotting the ACF, analysts can visualize how correlations decay as the lag increases, helping to uncover the temporal structure of the data. A slowly decaying ACF suggests a long memory process, where distant past values still exert influence on the present. In contrast, a rapidly diminishing ACF indicates a short memory process with more transient dependencies. Complementing the ACF is the partial autocorrelation function, or PACF, which measures the correlation between the time series and its lagged values after removing the effects of intermediate lags. The PACF is especially useful for identifying the order of autoregressive models, as it isolates the direct relationships at each lag.

Time series models are specifically designed to handle autocorrelation and make accurate forecasts by capturing the temporal dependencies in the data. The autoregressive model, or AR, expresses the current value of the series as a linear combination of its past values plus a random error term. The moving average model, or MA, models the current value as a function of past error terms. These two models can be combined into the autoregressive moving average model, or ARMA, which balances the strengths of both approaches. When the data is not stationary, meaning its statistical properties such as mean and variance change over time, differencing can be applied to stabilize the series. This leads to the autoregressive integrated moving average model, or ARIMA, which is one of the most widely used models in time series forecasting.

Stationarity is a crucial concept in time series analysis. A stationary time series has constant mean, variance, and autocovariance over time, making it more amenable to modeling and forecasting. Nonstationary data, which includes trends, seasonal effects, or structural changes, must often be transformed to achieve stationarity before applying traditional models. Common techniques include differencing, logarithmic transformation, and seasonal adjustment. Identifying whether a series is stationary can be done visually through plots or statistically through tests such as the Augmented Dickey-Fuller test, which evaluates the presence of a unit root indicating nonstationarity.

Seasonality is another key feature in many time series datasets, particularly those related to economics, climate, or retail. Seasonal patterns repeat at regular intervals and can be modeled explicitly through seasonal decomposition or incorporated into models such as the seasonal ARIMA, or SARIMA. Capturing seasonality accurately is critical for making reliable forecasts and understanding cyclical behavior. Exponential smoothing methods, including Holt-Winters smoothing, provide alternative approaches that weight recent observations more heavily and are particularly effective when the data exhibits both trend and seasonality.

Time series analysis also plays a significant role in model diagnostics and evaluation. After fitting a model, residual analysis is conducted to ensure that the remaining errors behave like white noise, meaning they are uncorrelated and have constant variance. Residual autocorrelation indicates that the model has not fully captured the structure in the data, suggesting the need for a more complex model or additional transformations. Tools such as the Ljung-Box test can formally assess whether residuals are free from autocorrelation, providing a statistical check on model adequacy.

In financial applications, autocorrelation analysis helps detect inefficiencies in markets, identify arbitrage opportunities, and model volatility through techniques like GARCH models. In environmental science, time series methods are used to monitor climate trends, forecast natural disasters, and evaluate the impact of human interventions. In industrial settings, time series models support quality control, predictive maintenance, and demand forecasting. The ubiquity of time-indexed data across disciplines highlights the importance of mastering autocorrelation and its implications for model design and interpretation.

Modern developments in time series analysis have introduced machine learning techniques capable of handling complex nonlinear dependencies and high-dimensional datasets. Recurrent neural networks, particularly long short-term memory models, excel at modeling long-range temporal dependencies and have revolutionized forecasting in fields like speech recognition and natural language processing. These methods implicitly capture autocorrelation and other temporal patterns without requiring the strict assumptions of classical models. Despite their flexibility, however, they require large amounts of data, careful tuning, and often sacrifice interpretability for performance.

Understanding autocorrelation is not only about identifying patterns but also about avoiding pitfalls in statistical analysis. Ignoring autocorrelation can result in underestimation of standard errors, inflated type I error rates, and poor forecast accuracy. Conversely, recognizing and modeling autocorrelation appropriately allows for more accurate predictions, better understanding of temporal dynamics, and more effective decision-making. Time series analysis, grounded in the study of autocorrelation, provides a rigorous framework for analyzing dynamic data and uncovering the underlying structure that governs change over time.

Causal Inference and Instrumental Variables

Causal inference is the discipline within statistics and econometrics that aims to answer questions about cause-and-effect relationships rather than simple associations. While traditional statistical models can reveal correlations between variables, these associations do not imply causality. To establish whether one variable truly influences another, it is necessary to account for potential confounders and ensure that the observed relationship is not driven by unmeasured factors or reverse causality. In observational data, where random assignment is not feasible, identifying causal effects becomes especially challenging. This is where techniques such as instrumental variables play a crucial role, providing a framework for estimating causal relationships in the presence of endogeneity.

Endogeneity arises when an explanatory variable is correlated with the error term in a regression model. This violation of the exogeneity assumption leads to biased and inconsistent estimates, undermining the validity of standard regression techniques. Endogeneity can result from omitted variable bias, measurement error, or simultaneity, where the dependent and independent variables influence each other. In such cases, the observed relationship cannot be interpreted as causal without addressing the source of bias. Instrumental variable (IV) methods offer a solution by introducing an external variable, known as the instrument, that influences the endogenous explanatory variable but is uncorrelated with the error term in the outcome equation.

An ideal instrument must satisfy two key conditions. The first is relevance, meaning the instrument must be correlated with the endogenous explanatory variable. Without this correlation, the instrument has no predictive power and cannot help isolate the variation needed to identify the causal effect. The second condition is the exclusion restriction, which requires that the instrument affects the dependent variable only through its influence on the endogenous explanatory variable and not through any other channel. This assumption is not directly testable and relies on theoretical justification, empirical plausibility, and contextual knowledge of the problem at hand.

Instrumental variable estimation typically proceeds in two stages. The first stage involves regressing the endogenous variable on the instrument and any other exogenous variables in the model. This produces predicted values of the endogenous variable that are purged of the endogenous component. In the second stage, the outcome variable is regressed on the predicted values obtained from the first stage. This two-stage least squares (2SLS) approach yields consistent estimates of the causal effect under the validity of the instrument. The strength of the instrument, as indicated by the first-stage F-statistic, is critical to the reliability of the results. Weak instruments, those that are only weakly correlated with the endogenous variable, can lead to imprecise estimates and large standard errors.

Instrumental variable techniques have been widely applied in economics, social sciences, epidemiology, and public policy. For instance, in estimating the return to education on wages, a common concern is that unobserved ability influences both education and earnings, confounding the relationship. To address this, researchers have used instruments such as proximity to colleges or changes in compulsory schooling laws. These instruments are assumed to influence education decisions without directly affecting earnings, allowing for a more credible estimate of the causal impact of education. Similarly, in health economics, randomized encouragement designs and physician prescribing preferences have served as instruments to study the effects of medical treatments where randomization is not possible.

The validity of an instrument is paramount, and extensive sensitivity analyses are often conducted to assess the robustness of the findings. Overidentification tests, such as the Sargan or Hansen test, can be used when there are more instruments than endogenous variables. These tests evaluate whether the instruments as a group are uncorrelated with the error term and thus satisfy the exclusion restriction. However, passing such tests does not prove the validity of each instrument individually and cannot compensate for fundamentally flawed instruments. Therefore, careful theoretical reasoning and domain expertise are indispensable in choosing and defending instruments.

Beyond linear models, instrumental variable techniques have been extended to non-linear settings and models with limited dependent variables. Control function approaches and generalized method of moments (GMM) estimation allow for greater flexibility in modeling complex relationships while still addressing endogeneity. These methods retain the core idea of using instruments to isolate exogenous variation and identify causal effects but adapt the estimation procedures to accommodate the specific characteristics of the data and the model structure.

In recent years, the use of natural experiments and quasi-experimental designs has revitalized interest in instrumental variables. Natural experiments exploit exogenous variation arising from institutional changes, policy reforms, or random events that mimic the conditions of randomized trials. When such variation satisfies the assumptions of relevance and exclusion, it provides a compelling source of identification for causal inference. The rise of these methods reflects a broader shift in empirical research toward designs that emphasize transparency, plausibility, and identification strategy.

Despite their power, instrumental variables are not a panacea for all endogeneity problems. The assumptions required for valid inference are strong and often unverifiable. The use of weak or invalid instruments can produce estimates that are worse than those obtained from biased ordinary least squares models. Moreover, the interpretation of IV estimates must be handled with care. In particular, when the instrument affects only a subset of the population, the estimated effect may be local to those whose treatment status is influenced by the instrument. This local average treatment effect (LATE) is informative but may not generalize to the broader population, underscoring the importance of understanding the nature of the instrument and its impact.

Causal inference remains one of the most challenging and consequential endeavors in empirical research. Instrumental variable methods offer a principled approach to addressing the limitations of observational data and uncovering the true effects of interventions, policies, and behaviors. By leveraging exogenous variation that is plausibly unrelated to confounders, these techniques make it possible to move beyond correlation and toward credible causal claims. The thoughtful application of IV methods requires not only technical competence but also deep contextual knowledge, critical thinking, and a commitment to transparent and rigorous analysis. As the demand for causal answers continues to grow across disciplines, instrumental variables remain a vital component of the empirical toolkit for researchers dedicated to understanding how the world truly works.

Hierarchical and Mixed Models

Hierarchical and mixed models are essential tools in modern statistics for analyzing data that possess a multilevel or nested structure. In many real-world scenarios, data are not independent observations drawn from a single homogeneous population but are instead grouped in ways that reflect the organization of the system being studied. Students are nested within classrooms, patients within hospitals, employees within companies, or repeated measures within individuals over time. Ignoring this structure and treating all observations as independent can lead to incorrect inferences, underestimated standard errors, and misleading conclusions. Hierarchical models, also known as multilevel models, and mixed models, which include both fixed and random effects, provide a principled framework for addressing such complexities.

The core idea behind hierarchical models is that data can be structured at multiple levels, with each level contributing its own sources of variation. For example, in educational research, test scores may depend not only on individual student characteristics but also on attributes of the classroom or teacher. A model that only considers individual-level predictors would overlook the influence of higher-level factors and fail to capture the dependencies within groups. Hierarchical models explicitly incorporate these levels by allowing for variation both within and between groups, thus providing a more accurate and nuanced understanding of the data.

Mixed models extend traditional regression models by including both fixed effects, which apply to the entire population or specific experimental conditions, and random effects, which account for the variability associated with different levels or groupings in the data. Fixed effects represent the average relationship between predictors and the outcome across the population, while random effects allow intercepts or slopes to vary across groups. This combination enables mixed models to capture heterogeneity in a flexible and statistically sound manner. For example, in a clinical trial conducted across multiple sites, a mixed model can account for differences in baseline health outcomes or treatment effects between sites, improving both precision and generalizability.

One of the key benefits of hierarchical and mixed models is their ability to borrow strength across groups. In a hierarchical Bayesian framework, for instance, group-level parameters are drawn from a common distribution, which allows information to be shared among groups. This regularization shrinks extreme estimates toward the overall mean, reducing the risk of overfitting in small groups and enhancing the stability of estimates. This feature is particularly valuable when some groups have limited data, as it prevents noisy estimates from dominating the analysis. In frequentist approaches, similar shrinkage can be observed through empirical Bayes estimates, which also moderate group-level estimates based on the overall distribution.

Estimation in hierarchical and mixed models can be computationally intensive, especially as the number of levels and random effects increases. Various methods have been developed to address these challenges, including maximum likelihood estimation, restricted maximum likelihood (REML), and Bayesian methods using Markov chain Monte Carlo (MCMC) techniques. Each approach has its advantages and trade-offs. REML, for example, provides unbiased estimates of variance components and is often preferred in small samples. Bayesian methods offer flexibility and the ability to incorporate prior information, but they require careful specification of priors and can be sensitive to convergence issues in complex models.

Model specification is a critical step in hierarchical modeling. Researchers must decide which effects should be treated as fixed and which as random, a decision that depends on the research question, the study design, and the data structure. Fixed effects are appropriate when the levels of a factor are of specific interest and exhaust the possibilities, such as treatment conditions in an experiment. Random effects are suitable when the levels represent a sample from a larger population, such as schools, hospitals, or regions. In some cases, a factor may include both fixed and random components, as when modeling random slopes for individual growth trajectories while estimating an average effect across the population.

Hierarchical models are particularly useful for analyzing longitudinal data, where repeated measurements are taken from the same subjects over time. In this context, observations are nested within individuals, and mixed models can accommodate both time-invariant and time-varying covariates, as well as random intercepts and slopes that capture individual trajectories. These models are robust to missing data under the assumption of missing at random and can handle irregular measurement intervals, making them ideal for studying change over time in real-world settings. The flexibility of hierarchical models in accommodating complex data structures has led to their widespread adoption in social sciences, education, public health, and biomedical research.

Interpretation of mixed models requires attention to both the fixed and random components. Fixed effects describe the average effect of predictors, while random effects quantify the variability around these averages. The variance components provide insights into the proportion of total variability attributable to different levels of the hierarchy. Intraclass correlation coefficients (ICCs) are commonly used to summarize the degree of similarity within groups, indicating how much of the variation is due to differences between groups rather than individuals. These measures help assess the appropriateness of hierarchical modeling and inform decisions about study design and sampling strategies.

Model comparison and validation are essential aspects of working with hierarchical and mixed models. Likelihood-based criteria such as the Akaike Information Criterion (AIC) and Bayesian Information Criterion (BIC) can be used to compare models with different fixed and random effects. Cross-validation and posterior predictive checks offer ways to evaluate model fit and predictive accuracy. Visual diagnostics, such as residual plots and plots of random effects, help identify model misspecification, outliers, or violations of assumptions such as normality and homoscedasticity. These tools are vital for ensuring that the model provides a faithful representation of the data and yields reliable inferences.

The power of hierarchical and mixed models lies in their capacity to handle the realities of nested data and account for multiple sources of variation simultaneously. By recognizing the layered structure of the data and modeling it explicitly, these models provide a richer and more accurate picture of the underlying processes. They enable researchers to explore not only average effects but also the variability and context in which these effects occur. This deeper understanding leads to more informed conclusions, better predictions, and more effective interventions. As datasets continue to grow in complexity and scale, hierarchical and mixed models remain indispensable tools for uncovering structure, explaining variability, and making sense of data that are anything but flat.